A Practical Grammar of the Italian Language

L. Mariotti

Copyright © BiblioBazaar, LLC

BiblioBazaar Reproduction Series: Our goal at BiblioBazaar is to help readers, educators and researchers by bringing back in print hard-to-find original publications at a reasonable price and, at the same time, preserve the legacy of literary history. The following book represents an authentic reproduction of the text as printed by the original publisher and may contain prior copyright references. While we have attempted to accurately maintain the integrity of the original work(s), from time to time there are problems with the original book scan that may result in minor errors in the reproduction, including imperfections such as missing and blurred pages, poor pictures, markings and other reproduction issues beyond our control. Because this work is culturally important, we have made it available as a part of our commitment to protecting, preserving and promoting the world's literature.

All of our books are in the "public domain" and many are derived from Open Source projects dedicated to digitizing historic literature. We believe that when we undertake the difficult task of re-creating them as attractive, readable and affordable books, we further the mutual goal of sharing these works with a larger audience. A portion of Bibliobazaar profits go back to Open Source projects in the form of a donation to the groups that do this important work around the world. If you would like to make a donation to these worthy Open Source projects, or would just like to get more information about these important initiatives, please visit www.bibliobazaar.com/opensource.

A

PRACTICAL GRAMMAR

OF THE

ITALIAN LANGUAGE;

FOR THE USE OF THE STUDENTS

OF

LONDON UNIVERSITY COLLEGE.

BY

L. MARIOTTI.

London:

P. ROLANDI, No. 20, BERNERS STREET.

MDCCCLI.

ADVERTISEMENT.

There is no English-Italian Grammar in common use in this country. Those generally placed in the student's hands—such as Vergani's—are mere translations of French-Italian Grammars, too often regardless of idiomatic peculiarities, either French or English.

The "Italian Grammar" published years ago, in the United States, by Pietro Bachi, teacher of Italian in Harvard University, a work of great merit, is utterly unknown in England; perhaps owing to its bulk—500 pages—perhaps also to the bigoted views of old-fashioned classicism, which prompted the author to choose his examples and his very exercises, almost exclusively from the writers of the fourteenth century, as if his object had been to train the English learner to write in the style of Boccaccio and his age.

Robello's "Grammaire Italienne" is also entitled to great respect: the writer, however, enters into inquiries more strictly belonging to universal than to special grammar; not a few of his remarks are original, all of them ingenious; but their soundness, and still more their pertinence, may be questioned.

The book is, moreover, only available for French pupils; for, notwithstanding the contrary opinion and practice of some schoolmistresses and certain instructors, we hold that a language should always be taught by the means of the tongue that comes more immediately home to the learner.

The present grammar is largely indebted to Robello's work : and we would have preferred to give merely an English version of the latter, had it been possible to undertake it without frequent and important modifications, which a proper regard for the author forbade.

The present work presupposes in the pupil the knowledge of general grammar. The common-place definitions of Nouns, Adjectives, &c., have been purposely omitted : the rules have been condensed within the narrowest limits of clearness and precision, and the practical advantages of the book will be found in the Examples and Exercises, which have also been reduced to the shortest sentences, so as to enable the pupil to comprehend them, and, if possible, to commit them to memory.

These few pages do not profess to teach " Italian " without a Master." On the contrary, the writer relies on the constant co-operation and direction of an able and intelligent Teacher.

21, THURLOE SQUARE,
LONDON, *October* 1851.

CONTENTS.

	Page
I.—PRONUNCIATION,	1

Vowels, 1-2 ;—Consonants, 3 ;—*c, sc, g*, 4-7 ;—*h*, 8 ;—*gl*, 9 ;—*gn*, 10 ;—*gu*, 11 ;—*qu*, 12 ;—*s*, 13 ;—*z*, 14 ;—*r*, 15 ; —Diphthongs, 16 ;—Double Consonants, 17 ;—Accent, 18.

II.—ARTICLES, ... 4

Definite Article, 4-7 ;—Indefinite Article, 8 ;—Prepositions, 9 ;—Articled Prepositions, 10 ;—Partitive Articles, 11 ; —Use of the Article, 12-13.

III.—GENDER OF NOUNS, ... 12

Nouns in *o*, 2 ;—in *a*, 3 ; in *e*, 4 ; in *i* and *u*, 5 ;—Peculiarities of Genders, 6.

IV.—PLURAL OF NOUNS, ... 16

Plural of Masculines, 1 ;—of Feminines, 3 ;—Nouns in *ca, ga, co, go, ia, io*, 3 ;—Irregular Plurals, 4-5 ;—Redundant Nouns, 6-8.

V.—ADJECTIVES, ... 19

Terminations of Adjectives, 1-4 ;—Their concordance, 5 ; —Their position, 6 ;—Peculiarities of Adjectives, 7.

VI.—COMPARATIVES AND SUPERLATIVES, . . . 23

Comparative of Superiority and Inferiority, 1 ;—of Equality, 2 ;—Relative Superlative, 3 ;—Absolute Superlative, 4 ;—Comparatives and Superlatives derived from Latin, 5.

VII.—AUGMENTATIVES AND DIMINUTIVES, ... 28

CONTENTS.

	Page
VIII.—NUMERAL ADJECTIVES,	31

Cardinal Numbers, 1-2;—Ordinal Numbers, 3-4;—Numeral Substantives, 5;—Peculiarities of Numbers, 6.

IX.—PERSONAL PRONOUNS, ... 35

Their Declension, 1;—Use of the Nominative, 2;—Conjunctive Pronouns, 3;—Their position, 4;—Their use, 5;—Double Pronouns, 6-7;—The Pronouns with Reflected Verbs, 8.

X.—POSSESSIVE PRONOUNS, ... 46

Their terminations, 1;—Their use, 2;—Peculiarities, 3.

XI.—DEMONSTRATIVE PRONOUNS, ... 49

Questo, cotesto, and *quello*, 1-2;—*Questo*, and *quello*, 3;—Substantive Pronouns, 4;—*Ciò, ciò che*, etc., 6.

XII.—RELATIVE PRONOUNS, ... 53

Quale, 1;—*Che, cui, chi*, 2-5;—*Onde*, 6;—Interrogative Pronouns, 9-12.

XIII.—INDEFINITE PRONOUNS, ... 57

Ogni, qualche, qualunque, 1;—*Ognuno*, etc., 2;—*Alcuno*, etc., 3;—*Tutto*, 4;—*Tale*, 5;—*Esso*, 6;—*Altro*, 7;—Peculiarities, 8.

XIV.—REGULAR VERBS, ... 61

General Remarks, 1-4;—Paradigm, 4.

XV.—AUXILIARY VERBS, ... 66

Avere and *essere*, 1; Compound Tenses, 2;—Active Verbs, 3;—Passive Verbs, 4; Agreement of Participles, 5-7; *Andare, stare, venire*, used as Auxiliaries, 8-9;—The Particle *si*, 10-11.

XVI.—MOODS AND TENSES, ... 72

Imperfect and Preterit, 1-4;—Compound Tenses, 5-7;—Use of the Subjunctive, 8;—of the Infinitive, 9;—of the Participle, 10-11.

XVII.—IRREGULAR VERBS; FIRST CONJUGATION, . . 80

General Remarks, 1-5;—Verbs in *care* and *gare*, in *ciare* and *giare*, etc., 6; *Andare, dare*, and *stare*, and their Compounds.

XVIII.—SECOND CONJUGATION, ... 85

Regular Verbs, their peculiarities, 1-3;—Irregular Preterits and Past Participles of Verbs in *acre*, in *bere*, in *cere*, in *dere*, in *gere*, in *guere*, in *lere*, in *gliere*, in *mere*, in *nere*, in *pere*, in *rere*, in *tere*, in *vere*, 4.

XIX.—SECOND CONJUGATION, CONTINUED, . . . 90

Trarre, 2;—*Condurre, dire, fare, piacere*, 3;—*Cadere, vedere, sedere*, 4.

CONTENTS.   vii

	Page
XX.—SECOND CONJUGATION, CONTINUED, ...	96

Spegnere, cingere, 1;—Valere, dolere, volere, solere, svellere, 2;—Scegliere, togliere, 3;—Rimanere, porre, tenere, 4;—Sapere, 5;—Parere, 6;—Potere, 7;—Dovere, bere, 8.

XXI.—THIRD CONJUGATION, ... 102

Regular Verbs, 1;—Verbs in *isco*, 2-3;—*Seguire*, 4;—*Salire*, 5;—*Apparire*, 6;—*Morire*, 7;—*Venire*, 8;—*Udire*, 9;—*Uscire*, 10;—*Cucire*, 11;—*Empire*, 12;—*Aprire*, 13, etc.

XXII.—DEFECTIVE VERBS, ... 107

Angere, 1;—*Algere*, 2;—*Arrogere*, 3; *Calere*, 4;—*Colere*, 5;—*Estollere*, 6;—*Fiedere*, 7;—*Gire*, 8;—*Ire*, 9;—*Licere*, 10, etc.

XXIII.—PREPOSITIONS, ... 109

Di, 1;—*A*, 2;—*Da*, 3;—*Per*, 4;—Con, 5;—*In*, 6;—Tra, 7;—Su, 8, etc.

XXIV.—ADVERBS, ... 117
XXV.—CONJUNCTIONS, ... 122
XXVI.—INTERJECTIONS, ... 126
XXVII.—CONSTRUCTION, ... 130

Inversions, 1-3—Ellipsis, 4-7;—Modes of Address, *Tu*, *Voi*, and *Ella*, 8-13.

Errata.

Page 7, line 26, for kitchen, *read* cellar.
Page 12, last line, for *a, o, u*, read *a, o, e.*
Page 13, line 28, for irregularities, *read* peculiarities.

ITALIAN GRAMMAR.

I.—PRONUNCIATION.

1. The Italian Language has five vowels, *a, e, i, o, u.*
2. Their approximate sounds in English are:

<table>
<tr><td>a</td><td colspan="2">father.</td><td>Ex. Pá-pa,</td><td>Pope.</td></tr>
<tr><td rowspan="2">e</td><td>{</td><td>fate.</td><td>vé-na,</td><td>vein.</td></tr>
<tr><td>{</td><td>fair.</td><td>ér-ba,</td><td>herb.</td></tr>
<tr><td>i</td><td colspan="2">meet.</td><td>ni-do,</td><td>nest.</td></tr>
<tr><td rowspan="2">o</td><td>{</td><td>rose.</td><td>vó-lo,</td><td>flight.</td></tr>
<tr><td>{</td><td>cause.</td><td>ló-de,</td><td>praise.</td></tr>
<tr><td>u</td><td colspan="2">root.</td><td>mú-to,</td><td>dumb.</td></tr>
</table>

(*a*) The *e* and *o* have a *close* and an *open* sound. The difference, however, is only perceptible when the accent of the word falls upon those vowels themselves, as in *véna, érba, vólo, lóde.* This difference cannot be reduced to any positive rule. Both vowels are open when accented at the end of the word, as in *te-mè,* he feared; *a-mò,* he loved. The *o* is generally open when it derives from a Latin *au,* as in *pó-sa,* pause (from *pausa*), and close when it derives from a Latin *v,* as in *vol-to,* face (from *vultus*).

(*b*) The *j* is not used in modern Italian editions. Its sound should be between that of *i* and *ii*.

3. The consonants *b, d, f, l, m, n, p, t, v,* are pronounced as in English.
4. The consonants *c, sc,* and *g,* have a *hard* sound before *a, o, u,* and a *soft* sound before *e* and *i*.
5. The hard sound of *c* is like the English *k,—ca,*

B

co, cu, ce, ci. The soft sound is somewhat like an English *ch*,—*ce, ci*.

6. The hard *sc*, sounds like the English *sk*,—*sca, sco, scu*. The soft sound resembles the English *sh*,—*sce, sci*.

7. The hard *g* is like the English *g* in the same syllables, *ga, go, gu*. The soft *g* is like the English *j* or *dg*,—*ge, gi*.

8. The *h* has no sound of its own. But it hardens the sound of *c, sc*, and *g*, in those cases in which those consonants would otherwise be soft.
Ex. *ce, che ; ci, chi ; sce, sche ; sci, schi ; ge, ghe ; gi, ghi*.

9. *Gl*, before *a, e, o, u*, is pronounced as in English. Ex. *gla, gle, glo, glu ;* before *i*, it has a peculiar sound, somewhat resembling the *ll* in the English words *brilliant, million*. Ex. *é-gli*, he ; *fi-glio*, son.

10. *Gn* has a peculiar sound, somewhat like *ni* in the words *union, onion ; gna, gne, gni, gno, gnu*. Ex. *dé-gno*, worthy.

11. *Gu*, in the syllables *gua, gue, gui, guo*, is pronounced as in the English words *anguish, languish*. Ex. *lin-gua*, tongue.

12. *Qu*, in the syllables *qua, que, qui, quo*, sounds as in the English words *vanquish, relinquish*. Ex. *é-quo*, equitable.

13. *S* may have either a *sibilant* sound, as in the English words *saint, hearse*, as *sán-to*, saint ; *pen-so*, I think ; or a somewhat softened sound, peculiar to the Italian, as *pò-sa*, pause ; *cò-sa*, thing.

(*a*) The soft sound occurs when the *s* is placed between vowels, as in *rì-so*, rice : *ro-sa*, rose ; and also before the consonants *b, d, g, l, m, n, r, v*. Ex. *sbá-glio*, mistake ; *sdé-gno*, disdain, &c. The sibilant sound occurs when the *s* is before vowels, at the beginning of a word, or preceded by a consonant, as in *se-ra*, evening ; *sèn-so*, sense ; before the consonants *c, f, p, q, t*, as in *sca-glia*, scale ; *sfi-da*, challenge, &c. ; also between vowels in compound words. Ex. *dìcesi (dìce-si*), they say ; *diségno (di-ségno*), design.

14. *Z* has a *hard* sound, somewhat like an English *ts*,

or *tz*, as in *sá-zio*, sated; *paz-zo*, fool: and a soft sound, somewhat like an English *ds*, or *dz*, as in *zi-o*, uncle; *méz-zo*, means.

(*a*) The *z* is hard when it derives from a Latin *t*, *ct*, or *pt*. Ex. *grá-zia*, grace (from gratia); *a-zió-ne*, action (from actio); *nóz-ze*, wedding (from nuptiæ). It is soft when derived from a Latin *d*. Ex. *róz-zo*, rude (from rudis); or from a Greek ζ, as in *zó-na*, zone; *o-riz-zonte*, horizon. It is *generally* hard after a consonant, as in *sén-za*, without.

15. The *r* has a peculiar sound, especially at the end of the syllables, *ar*, *er*, *ir*, *or*, *ur*, where the vowels, unlike in English, preserve their sounds in all their purity, *a-r*, *e-r*, &c.

16. Every letter is pronounced. Every vowel distinctly heard, even when two or three form but one syllable, as *ciò*, that; *può*, he can; *miei*, mine; *tuoi*, thine:—Compare *ce-lo*, I hide, with *cie-lo*, heaven.

17. Double consonants are pronounced with double emphasis.

(*a*) The mute consonants *b, c, d, p, q, t, v*, with two distinct and somewhat separate sounds, as *fát-to*, deed; the liquid *l, m, n, r*, the *f*, and *s*, with a continued sound, as *dăm-ma*, doe; *sĕr-ra*, saw. In all cases of double consonants, the preceding vowel acquires a shorter, sharper sound. Compare the above words with *fà-to*, fate; *dà-ma*, lady; *sé-ra*, evening. The soft double *c* as in *tác-cio*, I am silent, is pronounced somewhat like *tátch-chio*; the soft double *g* in *vég-gio*, I see, is pronounced like *védy-gio*.

18. Every word has an accent. Peculiar stress is laid on the accented vowel. Ex. *à-mŏ*, I love; *à-mă-nŏ*, they love. At the end of a word, the accented vowel has a short, sharp sound, as *ă-mò*, he loved.

(*a*) The position of the accent must be determined by practice. When it falls on the last syllable, the accent is always marked thus, *amò*, he loved. Most Italian words have the accent on the penultimate syllable, or last but one, fewer on the last but two, very few on the last but three. The accents have been marked on the following exercise.

Exercise.

chié-sa,   church.   slác-cio,   I untie.

ITALIAN GRAMMAR.

cióc-ca,	tuft.	á-e-re,	air.
cén-cio,	rag,	so-á-ve,	sweet.
cián-cia,	idle talk.	chic-che-ra,	cup.
strác-cio,	rag.	chiác-che-ra,	chat.
schiát-ta,	race.	záz-ze-ra,	mane.
ér-to,	steep.	zan-zá-ra,	gnat.
ir-to,	bristling.	e-só-so,	hated.
ór-to,	garden.	gen-gí-va,	gum.
úr-to,	shock.	gió-vi-ne,	youth.
áu-ra,	air.	schia-máz-zo,	clamour.
cí-gno,	swan.	au-ró-ra,	dawn.
ci-glio,	eyelid.	sog-ghi-gno,	grin.
giú-gno,	tune.	fi-gliuó-lo,	son.
gió-go,	yoke.	quan-tún-que,	although.
quál-che,	some.	pre-di-có,	he preached.
chec-chè,	whatever.	pre-di-co,	I foretell.
lég-ge,	law.	pré-di-co,	I preach.
ghi-gno,	grin.	pré-di-ca-no,	they preach.
ró-so,	gnawed.	scé-glie-re,	to choose.
rós-so,	red.	spé-gne-re,	to quench.
róz-zo,	rude.	frig-ge-re,	to fry.
véz-zo,	necklace.	ú-lu-la,	he howls.
guiz-zo,	quiver.	zé-fi-ro,	zephyr.
á-glio,	garlic.	a-é-re-o,	aerial.
scác-chi,	chess.	ca-pi-tá-no,	captain.
guér-ra,	war.	cá-pi-ta-no,	they happen.

———◆———

II.—ARTICLES.

1. The Italian Language has two genders, masculine and feminine ; and two numbers, singular and plural.
2. The cases are distinguished by articles and prepositions.
3. The articles are definite or indefinite.

ARTICLES.

4. The definite articles are *lo*, pl. *gli*; *il*, pl. *i*, for masculine nouns; *la*, pl. *le*, for feminine.

5. *Lo*, pl. *gli*, is used before masculine nouns beginning with *s* followed by a consonant; or beginning with *z*; or beginning with a vowel.

Ex.
lo spirito,	pl. gli spiriti,	the spirit.
lo zio,	gli zii,	the uncle.
l' amore,	gli amori,	the love.
l' errore,	gli errori,	the error.
l' onore,	gli onori,	the honour.
l' umore,	gli umori,	the humour.
l' Italiano,	gl' Italiani,	the Italian.

(*a*) *Lo* and *gli* are liable to elision—that is, to drop their final vowel and substitute an apostrophe, before vowels. With *lo* the elision may take place before all vowels: with *gli* only before *i*.

(*b*) With nouns beginning with *z*, the article *il*, pl. *i*, may also be used: *il zio*, pl. *i zii*.

6. *Il*, pl. *i*, is used before all other masculine nouns.
Ex. *il padre*, pl. *i padri*, the father.

(*a*) *Dio*, God, receives the article *gli*, instead of *i*, in the plural. Ex. *Il Dio*, the God; pl. *gli Dei*, the Gods.

7. *La*, pl. *le*, is used before all feminine nouns.

Ex.
la madre,	pl. le madri,	the mother.
l' anima,	le anime, or l' anime,	the soul.
l' ira,	le ire, or l' ire,	the anger.
l' ombra,	le ombre, or l' ombre,	the shade.
l' uva,	le uve, or l' uve,	the grape.
l' erba,	l' erbe,	the herb.

(*a*) *La* may suffer elision before all vowels. With *le* the elision is optional before *a*, *i*, *o*, *u*, but should be made before *e*.

8. The indefinite articles are *uno* and *una*. *Uno* is used before masculine nouns beginning with *s* followed by a consonant, or beginning by *z*. *Un* before all other masculine nouns. *Una* before feminine nouns beginning with a consonant; *un'* before all feminine nouns beginning with a vowel.

ITALIAN GRAMMAR.

Ex.	uno spirito,	a spirit.
	uno zio,	an uncle.
	un amore,	a love.
	una madre,	a mother.
	un' anima,	a soul.

9. The prepositions which are immediately connected with the declension of nouns are *di*, of; *a*, to or at; *da*, from or by; *in*, in; *con*, with; *su*, on, upon; *per*, for or by; *tra, fra*, among or between.

10. Articles and Prepositions combine in the declension as follows:—

Nominative or Accusative,			*lo*	*gli*	*il*		
Genitive,	of	*di*	*dello*	*degli*	*del*	*dei* or	*de'*
Dative,	to	*a*	*allo*	*agli*	*al*	*ai*	*a'*
Ablative,	from	*da*	*dallo*	*dagli*	*dal*	*dai*	*da'*
	in	*in*	*nello*	*negli*	*nel*	*nei*	*ne'*
	with	*con*	*collo*	*cogli*	*col*	*coi*	*co'*
	on	*su*	*sullo*	*sugli*	*sul*	*sui*	*su'*
	for	*per*	*per lo*	*per gli*	*pel*	*pei*	*pe'*
	among	*tra*	*tra lo*	*tra gli*	*tra 'l*	*trai*	*tra'*

Nominative or Accusative,			*la*	*le.*	*un* or *uno,*	*una.*
Genitive,	of	*di*	*della*	*delle.*	*d' un*	*d' una.*
Dative,	to	*a*	*alla*	*alle.*	*ad un*	*ad una.*
Ablative,	from	*da*	*dalla*	*dalle.*	*da un*	*da una.*
	in	*in*	*nella*	*nelle.*	*in un*	*in una.*
	with	*con*	*colla*	*colle.*	*con un*	*con una.*
	on	*su*	*sulla*	*sulle.*	*sur un*	*sur una.*
	for	*per*	*per la*	*per le.*	*per un*	*per una.*
	among	*tra*	*tra la*	*tra le.*	*tra un*	*tra una.*

(*a*) *Per* and *tra* only combine with *il* and *i*, *pel*, *pei*, not *pello*, *pegli*, etc.

(*b*) *Uno* and *una* only affect the prepositions *di*, *a*, and *su*. We may equally say *di un* or *d' un*, *a un* or *ad un*, *su un* or *sur un*, or *su d' un*.

Example.

del padre,   of the father.   dagli onori,   from the honours.

ARTICLES. 7

nello spirito,	in the spirit.	*per gl' Italiani,*	for the Italians.
alla madre,	to the mother.	*tra l' ombre,*	among the shades.
sull' anima,	on the soul.	*coll' erbe,*	with the herbs.
ad uno zio,	to an uncle.	*dei padri,*	of the fathers.
con un' ira,	with an anger.	*dalle madri,*	from the mothers.

11. The articles *dello, degli ; del, dei ; della, delle,* are used as partitive articles in the sense of *some, any, a few.*

Ex. *del pane,* some bread. *del vino,* any wine.
delle noci, a few nuts. *dei liquori,* liquors.

12. The articles are used in Italian upon general rules and principles analogous to the English.

Example.

Il *cavallo* dell' *Imperatore,* The Emperor's horse.
Un *cavallo* dell' *Imperatore,* A horse *of the* Emperor.
Il *cavallo* d'un *Imperatore,* The horse *of an* Emperor.

(a) However,—(i.)—The definite article is used in Italian when the noun is taken in a general and comprehensive sense.

Example.

L' *uomo nasce al lavoro,* Man is born to work.

(ii.)—It is used before the infinitive of verbs, before adjectives and adverbs when used substantively.

Example.

Il *cavalcare dà forza e coraggio,* Riding gives strength and spirit.
Il *dolce è misto all' amaro,* Sweetness is mixed with bitterness.
Vi *dirò il come e il perchè,* I'll tell you how and why.

(iii.)—On the contrary, the article may be omitted when the object is sufficiently determined by circumstances.

Example.

La *serva è* in *cantina,* The maid is in *the* kitchen.
Lo *zio era medico,* The uncle was *a* physician.

(iv.)—The definite article may be used before proper names of persons when an adjective or noun is sufficiently implied.

Example.

La *Caterina,* Catherine, meaning la bella *Caterina,* la cara *Caterina,* etc.
Il *Tasso,* Tasso, meaning il Poeta *Tasso,* il celebre *Tasso,* etc.

(v.)—The definite article is generally used before proper names of countries, when the whole country is comprehensively designated.

Example.

La *Lombardia è fertile,* Lombardy is fruitful.

13. The following examples may give some useful hints as to the use of the Articles:—

Example.

La *Provvidenza* del *Cielo,*	The Providence of Heaven.
Nel *fiore* della *gioventù,*	In the prime of youth.
Allo *spuntar* del *giorno,*	At day-break.
Cammino colle *stampelle,*	I walk with crutches.
L' *ozio è il padre di tutti i vizi,*	Idleness is the parent of all vices.
Gli *uomini son retti dal timore,*	Men are ruled by fear.
Attila, flagello di Dio,	Attila, *the* scourge of God.
Pio Nono, Pontefice regnante,	Pius *the* Ninth, *the* reigning Pope.
Le Commedie del *Goldoni,*	Goldoni's comedies.
La *Francia è irrequieta,*	France is restless.
Carlo Decimo, Re di Francia,	Charles *the* Tenth, King of France.
Ho viaggiato per Francia,	I have travelled about in France.
Ho viaggiato per la *Francia,*	I have travelled through France.
Vita di Torquato Tasso,	*A* life of Torquato Tasso.
Storia d' Italia, Libro Primo,	*The* History of Italy, Book *the* First.
Anch' io sono pittore,	I, too, am *a* painter.
Sulla scorza dei *faggi e* degli *allori,*	On the bark of beech trees and laurels.
Per monti e valli,	Over hills and dales.
Pei monti e per le *valli,*	Over the hills and dales.
Tra 'l marito e la moglie,	Between the husband and the wife.
Dal marito e dalla *moglie,*	From the husband and the wife.
Portami la *mia spada,*	Bring me my sword.
Ditelo a mia sorella,	Tell it to my sister.
Le *mie sorelle sono maritate,*	My sisters are married.

Exercise.

The master and the pupil. The king and the queen. The bridegroom and the bride. The hero and the heroine. The emperor and the empress. The prince and the princess. The altar and the victim. The ambassador.

Master, *maestro*, pl. *maestri*, m.; pupil, *scolare*, pl. *scolari*, m.; king, *re*, pl. *re*, m.; queen, *regina*, pl. *regine*, f.; bridegroom, *sposo*, pl. *sposi*, m.; bride, *sposa*, pl. *spose*, f.; hero, *eroe*, pl. *eroi*, m.; heroine, *eroina*, pl. *eroine*, f.; emperor, *imperatore*, pl. *imperatori*, m.; empress, *imperatrice*, pl. *imperatrici*, f.; prince, *principe*, pl. *principi*, m.; princess, *principessa*, pl. *principesse*, f.; altar, *altare*, pl. *altari*, m.; victim, *vittima*, pl. *vittime*, f.; ambassador, *ambasciatore*, pl. *ambasciatori*, m.

A king and a queen. The ambassadors. The heroes. The heroines. The hymns. The emperors. The zeal. The pupils and the masters. The friends. The nettles. The beauty. The universe. The flowers. The gardens.

Hymn, *inno*, pl. *inni*, m.; zeal, *zelo*, m.; friend, *amico*, pl. *amici*, m.; *amica*, pl. *amiche*, f.; nettle, *ortica*, pl. *ortiche*, f.; beauty, *bellezza*, pl. *bellezze*, f.; universe, *universo*, m.; flower, *fiore*, pl. *fiori*, m.; garden, *giardino*, pl. *giardini*, m.

The king's friend. The queen's friends. The master's stick. The emperor's son. The queen's garden. With the empress's children. From the beauty of the universe. In the hours of the morning. Among the flowers of the garden.

Stick, *bastone*, pl. *bastoni*, m.; son, *figlio*, pl. *figli*, m.; child, *fanciullo*, pl. *fanciulli*, m.; hour, *ora*, pl. *ore*, f.; morning, *mattina*, pl. *mattine*, f.

The keys of the garden door. On the garden door. The emperor's flatterers. The hymn of the prophet. With the hymns of the Lord. The king's uncle. The queen's aunts. The prince's uncles. An uncle of the princess.

Key, *chiave*, pl. *chiavi*, f.; door, *uscio*, pl. *usci*, m.; garden (kitchen-garden), *orto*, pl. *orti*, m.; flatterer, *adulatore*, pl. *adulatori*, m.; prophet, *profeta*, pl. *profeti*, m.; Lord, *Signore*, pl. *Signori*, m.; uncle, *zio*, pl. *zii*, m.; aunt, *zia*, pl. *zie*, f.

An hour. On a door. From a garden. On the door of a garden. With a stick. With the master's stick. The beauty of a child. Between the king and the queen. From the friends of the king. To the child's friends. Cæsar's friends. Cato's enemies. From Rome to Babylon.

Cæsar, *Cesare*, m.; Cato, *Catone*, m.; enemy, *nemico*, pl. *nemici*, m.; Rome, *Roma*, f.; Babylon, *Babilonia*, f.

The seasons of the year. The days of the week. In the hollow of the hand. On the street. To the post. With the carriage. In the inkstand. On the roof. Of the man. To the woman. With the men. From the women. Of a man. To a woman. With the women. From the men.

Season, *stagione*, pl. *stagioni*, f.; year, *anno*, pl. *anni*, m.; day, *giorno*, pl. *giorni*, m.; hollow, *concavo*, m.; hand, *mano*, pl. *mani*, f.; street, *strada*, pl. *strade*, f.; post, *posta*, f.; carriage, *carrozza*, pl. *carrozze*, f.; inkstand, *calamaio*, pl. *calamai*, m.; roof, *tetto*, pl. *tetti*, m.; man, *uomo*, pl. *uomini*, m.; woman, *donna*, pl. *donne*, f.

The day of judgment. The fear of death. The king's anger. The soul of the universe. By heaven's providence. The shadow of the tree. The shadows of the clouds. Among the grass and flowers. Heroes despise honours and pleasures. Some flowers. Some grass.

Judgment, *giudizio*, m.; fear, *timore*, m.; death, *morte*, f.; anger, *ira*, f.; soul, *anima*, f.; universe, *universo*, m.; heaven, *cielo*, m.; providence, *providenza*, f.; shadow, *ombra*, pl. *ombre*, f.; tree, *albero*, pl. *alberi*, m.; cloud, *nube*, pl. *nubi*, f.; grass, *erba*, pl. *erbe*, f.; honour, *onore*, pl. *onori*, m.; pleasure, *piacere*, pl. *piaceri*, m.; despise, *disprezzano*.

God is the judge of men's deeds. The snake in the grass. For heaven's sake. The church bells. The moonlight. At sunrise. On the top of the Alps. The mountains of the moon. The sands of the desert. The dust of the fields.

God, *Dio*, pl. *Dei*, m.; judge, *giudice*, pl. *giudici*, m.; deed, *azione*, pl. *azioni*, f.; snake, *angue*, m.; sake, *amore*, m.; church, *chiesa*, pl. *chiese*, f.; bell, *campana*, pl. *campane*, f.; moon, *luna*, f.; light, *lume*, m.; sunrise, *spuntar del sole*, m.; top, *cima*, pl. *cime*, f.; Alp, *Alpe*, pl. *Alpi*, f.; mountain, *monte*, pl. *monti*, m.; sand, *arena*, pl. *arene*, f.; desert, *deserto*, pl. *deserti*, m.; dust, *polve*, f.; field, *campo*, pl. *campi*, m.; is, *é*.

The remedy of evils. The garden of Europe. Moliere's works, volume the third. Slow to love and to anger. The fields and the meadows. In the fields and meadows. Through the fields and meadows. Along the fields and meadows.

Remedy, *rimedio*, pl. *rimedi*, m.; evil, *male*, pl. *mali*, m.; Europe, *Europa*, f.; work, *opera*, pl. *opere*, f.; volume, *tomo*, pl. *tomi*, m.; third, *terzo;* meadow, *prato*, pl. *prati*, m.; slow, *lento;* through, *per;* along, *lungo*.

Death is the end of evils. Italy is the garden of Europe. Milton, the English poet. Pope, also a poet. America was discovered by the Italians. The king is in the parlour. The queen is in the garden. London is the metropolis of England. Charles the First, King of England.

End, *termine*, m.; Italy, *Italia*, f.; English poet, *poeta Inglese*, m.; America, *America*, f.; Italian, *Italiano*, pl. *Italiani*, m.; parlour, *sala*, pl. *sale*, f.; London, *Londra*, f.; metropolis, *capitale*, f.; England, *Inghilterra*, f.; Charles, *Carlo*, m.; first, *primo*, m.

12   ITALIAN GRAMMAR.

Also, anch' egli; was discovered, fu scoperta; is, è.
On the banks of the stream. Along the sea-shore. I read with spectacles. I write with steel pens. In the heart of summer. From the fury of fortune. Men's passions. Women's whims. Castles in the air. Children's playthings.

Bank, *sponda*, pl. *sponde*, f. ; stream, *rio*, m. ; shore, *riva*, pl. *rive*, f. ; sea, *mare*, pl. *mari*, m. ; spectacles, *occhiali*, pl. m. ; pen, *penna*, pl. *penne*, f. ; steel, *acciaio*, m. ; heart, *cuore*, m. ; summer, *state*, f. ; fury, *furore*, m. ; fortune, *fortuna*, f. ; passion, *passione*, pl. *passioni*, f. ; whim, *capriccio*, pl. *capricci*, m. ; castle, *castello*, pl. *castelli*, m. ; air, *aria*, f. ; child (baby), *bambino*, pl. *bambini*, m. ; plaything, *trastullo*, pl. *trastulli*, m.

I read, *leggo*; I write, *scrivo*.

The queen is in the country. The king is not at home. The father is in town. The maid is in the cellar. We are going to the theatre. She is gone to church. The mother is at church. The children are at school. The children are going to school.

Country, *campagna*, f. ; home, *casa*, f. ; town, *città*, f. ; maid, *fantesca*, f. ; cellar, *cantina*, f. ; theatre, *teatro*, m. ; church, *chiesa*, f. ; father, *padre*, pl. *padri*, m. ; mother, *madre*, pl. *madri*, f. ; child, *fanciullo*, pl. *fanciulli*, m. ; school, *scuola*, f.

Is, *è*; is not, *non è*; at, *in*; we are going, *andiamo*; she is gone, *è andata*; are going, *vanno*.

———◆———

III.—GENDER OF NOUNS.

1. All Italian nouns end by a vowel. Most of them by *a, o, u.*

2. Nouns in *o* are masculine, as *il maestro*, the master; *il libro*, the book.

(*a*) Except *la mano*, the hand; and a few proper names of women, as *Saffo*, Sappho; *eco*, echo, &c.

3. Nouns in *a* are feminine, as *la sposa*, the bride; *la carta*, the paper.

(*a*) Except,—(i.)—Proper names of men, as *Andrea*, Andrew.

(ii.)—Names of men's dignities, offices, and professions, as *il papa*, the pope; and so *duca*, duke; *poeta*, poet; *profeta*, prophet; *artista*, artist; *giornalista*, journalist.

(iii.)—Nouns chiefly from a neuter Greek, as *il clima*, the climate; and so *stemma*, escutcheon; *dramma*, *poema*, *problema*, *epigramma*; *scisma*, schism; *pianeta*, planet; *monarca*, monarch, &c.

4. The gender of nouns in *e* cannot be reduced to general rules.

(*a*) However,—(i.)—Nouns in *ore* are masculine, as *lo splendore*, the splendour; *il dolore*, sorrow, &c.

(ii.)—Nouns in *udine*, *uggine*, *zione*, and most of those in *ione*, are feminine, as *la solitudine*, solitude; *la ruggine*, rust; *la nazione*, the nation; *l' unione*, the union, &c. &c.

5. Nouns in *i* and *u* are very few, their gender cannot be determined by rule.

(*a*) Those in *i* are mostly masculine, as *il pari*, the peer; except *la crisi*, the crisis; *la tesi*, the thesis; *la sintassi*, the syntax; *la metropoli*, the metropolis.

Those in *u* are generally feminine, as *la virtù*, virtue; *la tribù*, the tribe. Except *Gesù*, Jesus; *il Perù*, Peru.

6. The following irregularities with regard to the gender of nouns require some attention.

(*a*) Some nouns of animals and some applicable to human beings, change their gender by merely changing their termination, as *il cervo*, the stag; *la cerva*, the hind; and so *colombo*, and *colomba*, dove, &c. &c.; *il fanciullo*, the boy; *la fanciulla*, the girl; *il cuoco*, *la cuoca*, cook; *il fattore*, *la fattora*, steward, stewardess; *uno Spagnuolo*, a Spaniard; *una Spagnuola*, a Spanish woman, &c.

(*b*) Other similar nouns may have different genders with the same termination. Ex. *il lepre* and *la lepre*, the hare; *il serpe* and *la serpe*, the snake; *il giovine*, *la giovine*, the young man, the young woman; *un Francese*, a Frenchman; *una Francese*, a Frenchwoman, &c.

(c) Other similar nouns, again, have irregular terminations in the feminine, as *leone*, lion; *leonessa*, lioness; *conte*, count; *contessa*, &c.

(d) Some masculine nouns in *tore*, have their feminine in *trice*, as *autore*, author; *autrice*, authoress; *traditore*, traitor; *traditrice*, traitress, &c.

(e) Some nouns of trees, masculine, in *o*, change their termination in *a* and become feminine, to express the fruit. Ex. *il pero*, the pear-tree; *una pera*, a pear.

(f) Some nouns are masculine when terminated in *o*, and feminine when in *a*, as *il casato*, or *la casata*, the family name; and so *cioccolato*, chocolate; *cesto*, basket; *mattino*, morning; *orecchio*, ear; *scritto*, writing; *soffitto*, ceiling; all of which can equally be used as feminine, *cioccolata, cesta, mattina*, &c. &c.

(g) Some nouns may be used in both genders with the same termination, so *il carcere*, or *la carcere*, the prison; and so *trave*, beam; *folgore*, thunderbolt; *fine*, end; *fune*, rope; *gregge*, flock; *cenere*, ashes, &c.

Exercise.

The fear of God. The spirit of the Gospel. The hand of Providence. The mist of the evening. The water of the sea. The season of Lent. From the fury of the people. On the altar of the country. In the Prophet's book.

Fear, *timore*; God, *Dio*; spirit, *spirito*; gospel, *vangelo*; hand, *mano*; Providence, *Provvidenza*; mist, *nebbia*; evening, *sera*; water, *acqua*; sea, *mare*; season, *stagione*; Lent, *Quaresima*; fury, *furore*; people, *popolo*; altar, *altare*; country, *patria*; book, *libro*; prophet, *profeta*.

The fountain of truth. The love of virtue. For the climate of the south. The mother and the child. A flock of sheep. A peer of the realm. The lord's house. The poet's fury. A schism in the church. The king's coat-of-arms.

Fountain, *fonte*; truth, *verità*; love, *amore*; virtue, *virtù*; climate, *clima*; south, *mezzogiorno*; mother, *madre*; child, *fanciullo*; flock, *gregge*; sheep, *pecora*, pl. *pecore*; peer, *pari*; realm, *regno*; lord, *signore*; house, *casa*; poet, *poeta*; fury, *furia*; schism, *scisma*; church, *chiesa*; king, *re*; coat-of-arms, *stemma*.

GENDER OF NOUNS.

The monarch's diadem. The hymn of the prophet. The election of the pope gave rise to a schism. With the song of the poet. The fan of a Spanish woman. The coquetry of a French woman.

Monarch, *monarca;* diadem, *diadema;* hymn, *inno;* election, *elezione;* pope, *papa;* song, *canto;* fan, *ventaglio;* Spanish, *Spagnuolo;* coquetry, *civetteria;* French, *Francese;* gave rise to, *produsse.*

The strength of a bear. The bear and her young. The swiftness of a hare. The hare and her young. The brother is my friend. The sister is my friend. A country-man and a country-woman. The young man and the young woman.

Strength, *forza;* bear, *orso;* her young, *i suoi orsatti;* swiftness, *prestezza;* hare, *lepre;* her young, *i suoi lepratti;* brother, *fratello;* sister, *sorella;* friend, *amico;* my, *mio,* f. *mia;* country-man, *contadino;* young man, *giovine.*

The son and the daughter. The beauty of a Circassian (woman). The boy and the girl. The nephew and the niece. The bridegroom and the bride. The baron and the baroness. The duke and the duchess. The prince and the princess. The uncle and the aunt. The grandfather and the grandmother.

Son, *figlio;* beauty, *bellezza;* Circassian, *Circasso;* boy. *ragazzo;* nephew, *nipote;* bridegroom, *sposo;* baron. *barone;* duke, *duca;* prince, *principe;* uncle, *zio;* grandfather, *nonno.*

The marquis and the marchioness. The lord and the lady. The poet and the poetess. The prophet and the prophetess. The steward and the stewardess. Give me a pear and a peach.

Marquis, *marchese;* lord, *signore;* poet, *poeta;* prophet, *profeta;* steward, *fattore;* pear-tree, *pero;* peach-tree. *pesco;* give me, *datemi.*

IV.—PLURAL OF NOUNS.

1. Masculine nouns have their plural in *i*, as *maestro*, pl. *maestri*; *poeta, poeti*; *splendore, splendori*.

2. Feminine nouns in *a* have their plural in *e*, as *sposa*, pl. *spose*.

3. Feminine nouns in *e* have their plural in *i*, as *madre, madri*.

(*a*) Feminine nouns in *ca* and *ga* have their plurals in *che* and *ghe*, as *monaca, nun, monache*; *lega*, league, *leghe*.

(*b*) Masculine nouns in *co* and *go*, of two syllables, have their plural in *chi* and *ghi*, as *bosco*, wood, *boschi*; *lago*, lake, *laghi*.

Except *porco*, pig, pl. *porci*; *Greco*, Greek, *Greci*.

(*c*) Masculine nouns in *co* and *go*, of more than two syllables, have their plural in *chi* and *ghi* when the final syllable *co* and *go* is preceded by a consonant,—as *bifolco*, ploughman, *bifolchi*; *albergo*, inn, *alberghi*: they have their plural in *ci* and *gi* when the final syllable is preceded by a vowel, as *medico*, physician, *medici*; *teologo*, theologian, *teologi*.

The rule (*c*) is subject to frequent exceptions.

(*d*) Masculine nouns in *io* form their plural according to the common rule when the accent falls on the *i*,—as *zío*, uncle, *zii*: when the accent does not fall on the *i*, they form the plural by merely dropping the *o*,—as *spécchio*, mirror, *specchi*; *ràggio*, ray, *raggi*; *libràio*, bookseller, *librai*; *artíglio*, claw, *artigli*, &c. &c.

Some of them, however, especially such as might be mistaken for other words of different meaning, change the *io* into *j*, or into *ii*,—as *tempio*, temple, *tempj*, or *tempii*, to distinguish it from *tempi*, plural of *tempo*, time. So likewise *principio*, principle, *principj*, or *principii*, to distinguish it from *principi*, princes: also *studio*, study, pl. *studj* or *studii*, &c. Some write *tempî*, *principî*, *studî*.

(*e*) Feminine nouns in *cia* and *gia* follow the common rule if the accent falls upon the *i*,—as *farmacía*, apothecary's shop, *farmacie*; *bugia*, lie, *bugie*.

When the accent does not fall on the *i*, they generally change the *ia* into *e*, as *guáncia*, cheek, *guánce*; *gréggia*, flock, *gregge*.

4. Some nouns have irregular plurals, as *uomo*, man, *uomini*; *il Dio*, the God, *gli Dei*; *bue*, ox, *buoi*; *moglie*, wife, *mogli*, &c.

5. Nouns ending with an accented vowel, nouns in *i*

and *u*, and some few in *ie* (chiefly from the fifth declension of the Latin), have the same termination for both numbers; as *il re*, the king, *i re; la città*, city, *le città; la crisi*, crisis, *le crisi;* and so *tribù*, tribe; *specie*, species, &c. &c.

6. Some masculine nouns have, besides their regular plural in *i*, another feminine termination, in *a* (derived from a plural neuter in Latin), as *il labbro*, lip, *i labbri*, and *le labbra*: so, *anello*, ring; *castello*, castle; *coltello*, knife; *filo*, thread; *fuso*, spindle; *grido*, cry; *osso*, bone; *sacco*, sack; *quadrello*, arrow; *vestigio*, footprint, &c. &c.

(*) The nouns *labbro*, lip; *ciglio*, eyelid; *braccio*, arm; *dito*, finger; *calcagno*, heel; *gomito*, elbow; *ginocchio*, knee, &c. referring to parts of the human body, prefer the feminine termination, *labbra*, *ciglia*, *braccia*, &c.

(*b*) *Membra*, pl. of *membro*, means limbs, and refers to the body of man or animal; *membri* is also used for limbs, but more generally for members of a social body: so, *I membri del Parlamento*, the members of Parliament, not *le membra*.

(*o*) *Mura*, pl. of *muro*, wall, refers to the walls of bastions of town or castle; *muri* to the walls of house or room.

(*d*) *Corna*, pl. of *corno*, horn, is used for the horns of animals; *corni* for horns, musical instruments.

7. Some masculine nouns have only the feminine plural in *a*, as *l' uovo*, the egg, pl. *le uova*, the eggs; so, *miglio*, mile; *paio*, pair; *staio*, bushel; *centinaio*, a hundred; *migliaio*, a thousand, &c.

8. There are nouns redundant in the singular, as *sentiero* and *sentiere*, path, pl. *sentieri*; so *cavaliero* and *cavaliere*; *scolaro* and *scolare*, &c.

Nouns redundant in both numbers, as *arma* and *arme*, weapon, pl. *arme* and *armi*; so *vesta*, dress; *dota*, dower, &c.

Nouns used only in the singular, as *mele*, honey. Nouns only used in the plural, as *nozze*, wedding; *cesoie*, scissors, &c.

Exercise.

The idols of the Egyptians. The gods of the Greeks. The arms of providence. The rays of the sun. Among the antiquities of Greece. The land of woods and lakes. Fools are often the victims of rogues.

Idol, *idolo* ; Egyptian, *Egiziano* ; God, *Dio* ; Greek, *Greco* ; arm, *braccio* ; providence, *provvidenza* ; ray, *raggio* ; sun, *sole* ; antiquity, *antichità* ; Greece, *Grecia* ; land, *paese* ; wood, *bosco* ; lake, *lago* ; fool, *sciocco* ; victim, *vittima* ; rogue, *malvagio* ; are often, *sono spesso.*

The tribes of the Indians. The lips of the negroes. The scissors of the Fates. Flocks of pigs and geese. Mushrooms grow in the woods. Figs do not grow in the climates of the north. A grove of oranges.

Tribe, *tribù* ; Indian, *Indiano* ; lip, *labbro* ; negro, *negro* ; scissors, *cesoie* ; fate, *Parca* ; flock, *greggia* ; pig, *porco* ; goose, *oca* ; mushroom, *fungo* ; fig, *fico* ; climate, *clima* ; north, *settentrione* ; grove, *boschetto* ; orange, *arancio* ; grow, *nascono* ; do not grow, *non nascono.*

The diadems of the monarchs. The prophets of the Hebrews. The colour of the cheeks. The shops are under the porticoes. The curtains with fringes and tassels. The rays of the planets. The peers of the realm. The years of youth.

Diadem, *diadema* ; monarch, *monarca* ; prophet, *profeta* ; Hebrew, *Ebreo* ; colour, *colore* ; cheek, *guancia* ; shop, *bottega* ; portico, *portico* ; curtain, *cortina* ; fringe, *frangia* ; tassel, *fiocco* ; planet, *pianeta* ; peer, *pari* ; realm, *regno* ; year, *anno* ; youth, *gioventù* ; are under, *sono sotto.*

The chairs of the judges. The iniquity of men's judgments. The king's enemies. Jupiter's eyebrows. Father of men and gods. In the cities of the plain. The Scythians fought with bows and arrows. The wives of the Indians. The eggs of an ostrich.

Chair, *scanno* ; judge, *giudice* ; iniquity, *iniquità* ; judgment, *giudicio* ; man, *uomo* ; enemy, *nemico* ; king, *re* ; Jupiter, *Giove* ; eyebrow, *ciglio* ; city, *città* ; plain, *pianura* ; Scythian, *Scita* ; bow, *arco* ; arrow, *freccia* ; wife, *moglie* ; egg, *uovo* ; ostrich, *struzzo* ; fought, *combattevano*.

Two antlers on the door. On the walls of the city. Two herds of oxen. In the times of Queen Elizabeth. The temples of the gods. Coats-of-arms hang on the walls of the church The uprightness of the king's intentions. Sappho's poems.

Antler, *corno di cervo* ; door, *uscio* ; wall, *muro* ; herd, *mandra* ; ox, *bue* ; time, *tempo* ; Elizabeth, *Elisabetta* ; temple, *tempio* ; coat-of-arm, *stemma* ; church, *chiesa* ; uprightness, *rettitudine* ; intention, *intenzione* ; poem, *poema* ; Sappho, *Saffo* ; hang on, *pendono da*.

The wands of the magicians. The lies of the journalists. Two kinds of mushrooms. The egg of Columbus. To the sound of horns and flutes. The members of the senate. Midas had ass's ears. The cries of the child.

Wand, *verga* ; magician, *mago* ; lie, *bugia* ; journalist, *giornalista* ; kind, *specie* ; mushroom, *fungo* ; egg, *uovo* ; Columbus, *Colombo* ; sound, *suono* ; horn, *corno* ; flute, *flauto* ; member, *membro* ; senate, *senato* ; Midas, *Mida* ; ass, *asino* ; ear, *orecchio* ; cry, *grido* ; child, *fanciullo* ; had, *aveva*.

V.—ADJECTIVES.

1. All adjectives end in *o* or in *e*, as *dotto*, learned ; *prudente*, prudent.

2. Adjectives in *o* have four terminations : two for the singular, *dotto*, feminine *dotta* ; and two for the plural, *dotti*, feminine *dotte*.

3. Adjectives in *e* have two terminations : one for the

singular, *prudente*, masculine and feminine ; and one for the plural, *prudenti*, masculine and feminine.

(*a*) *Pari*, equal; and *impari*, unequal; the only adjectives in *i*, have only one termination for all genders and numbers.

4. In the formation of plurals, adjectives follow the same rules as nouns.

Ex. *Uomo dotto e prudente* ; —*uomini dotti e prudenti* ;— learned and prudent man–men. *Donna dotta e prudente* ;—*donne dotte e prudenti* ;—learned and prudent woman–women. *Principe ricco e saggio* ;—*principi ricchi e saggi*;—rich and wise prince–princes. *Principessa ricca e saggia* ;—*Principesse ricche e sagge* ;—rich and wise princess–princesses.

5. Adjectives agree with the nouns in gender and number.

Example.

il marito é pazzo,	the husband is mad.
la moglie è pazza,	the wife is mad.
padre e figlio son pazzi,	father and son are mad.
madre e figlia son pazze,	mother and daughter are mad.
marito e moglie son pazzi,	husband and wife are mad.

6. Adjectives are placed sometimes before, sometimes after the nouns, sometimes at a great distance.

Example.

eterna infamia,
infamia eterna, } eternal disgrace.

i raggi del sole sono benefici,
benefici sono i raggi del sole, } the rays of the sun are blissful.

(*a*) However, adjectives of taste, colour, shape, &c. are generally placed after the nouns.

Ex.		
	mandorle dolci,	sweet almonds.
	un drappo nero,	a black cloth.
	la tavola rotonda,	the round table.
	acqua fresca,	cold water.
	in lingua Latina,	in the Latin tongue.

(*b*) When two or more adjectives are added to the same noun, they are generally placed after the noun.

ADJECTIVES.

Example.

generale ardito ed intraprendente, a bold and enterprising general.
(These rules are often disregarded, especially in poetry.)

7. The following examples deserve attention:—

molta polve,	much dust, a great deal of dust.
molte gioie,	many jewels.
tanto orgoglio,	so much pride.
tanta viltà,	so much baseness.
tanti sciocchi,	so many fools.
tante volte,	so many times.
troppo rigore,	too much rigour.
troppa bontà,	too much goodness.
troppe ceremonie,	too many ceremonies.
poco senno,	little sense.
poca esperienza,	little experience.
pochi quattrini,	few farthings (little money).
poche difficoltà,	few difficulties.
quanto fumo!	how much smoke!
quanta canaglia!	what a rabble!
quanti raggiri!	how many intrigues!
quante bugie!	how many lies!
altrettanti soldati,	as many soldiers.
altrettante signore,	as many ladies.
bel giardino,	fine garden.
bello spirito,	fine wit.
bell' ingegno,	fine genius.
bei giardini,	fine gardens.
begli spiriti,	fine wits.
begl' ingegni,	fine geniuses.
gran birbone,	great rogue.
grande strepito,	great noise.
grand' amore,	great love.
gran regina,	great queen.
grande strage,	great slaughter.
grand' anima,	great soul.
buon vino,	good wine.

22   ITALIAN GRAMMAR.

buono stromento,   good instrument.
San Pietro,   St. Peter.
Santo Stefano,   St. Stephen.
Sant' Andrea,   St. Andrew.
Sant' Agata,   St. Agatha.
Santa Maria,   St. Mary.

Exercise.

A free and independent nation. The free cities of the Rhine. Blue eyes and black hair. The faint ray of the distant stars : of the wandering comets : of the wandering planets. The study of the Italian language

Nation, *popolo* ; free, *libero* ; independent, *indipendente* ; city, *città* ; Rhine, *Reno* ; eye, *occhio* ; blue, *azzurro* ; hair, *capelli* (plural) ; black, *nero* ; ray, *raggio* ; faint, *fioco* ; star, *stella* ; distant, *remoto* ; comet, *cometa* ; planet, *pianeta* ; wandering, *errante* ; study, *studio* ; language, *lingua* ; Italian, *Italiano*.

The Knights of the Round Table. The father is rich. The mother is rich. Father and son are rich. Mother and daughter are rich. The father and mother are blind to the faults of the daughter. A glass of cold water.

Knight, *cavaliere* ; table, *tavola* ; round, *rotondo* ; father, *padre* ; rich, *ricco* ; mother, *madre* ; son, *figlio* ; daughter, *figlia* ; blind, *cieco* ; fault, *difetto* ; glass, *bicchiere* ; water, *acqua* ; cold, *fresco* ; is, *è* ; are, *sono*.

Wrapt in a green cloak. The beautiful creature in (a) white robe. I have a fine horse. A black knight on a white steed. I have bought four beautiful horses. The church is large. A large church. St. Peter's church is a fine building.

Wrapt, *avvolto* ; green, *verde* ; cloak, *manto* ; beautiful, *bello* ; creature, *creatura* ; robe, *veste* ; white, *bianco* ; horse, *cavallo* ; fine, *bello* ; steed, *destriero* ; four, *quattro* ; church, *chiesa* ; large, *grande* ; Peter, *Pietro* ; building, *edifizio* ; I have, *ho* ; bought, *comprato*.

In Rome are many churches. So many churches ! How

many churches! Too many palaces! Many palaces and few churches. A great house. A great street. A fine palace. A fine tower. Many fine palaces.

Rome, *Roma;* palace, *palazzo;* house, *casa;* street, *strada;* tower, *torre;* are, *sono.*

A great talker! A great ass! The false Gods of the ancient Romans. The idols of the Greeks were blind and deaf. St. Anthony is the patron of pigs. The mornings are cool. The evenings are short. The days are long. St. Lucy's street.

Talker, *ciarlone;* ass, *asino;* false, *bugiardo;* ancient, *antico;* Roman, *Romano;* idol, *idolo;* Greek, *Greco;* deaf, *sordo;* blind, *cieco;* Anthony, *Antonio;* patron, *protettore;* pig, *porco;* morning, *mattinata;* cool, *fresco;* evening, *serata;* short, *corto;* day, *giornata;* long, *lungo;* Lucy, *Lucia;* street, *strada.*

So much baseness! So many crimes! How many traitors? Too many cooks! So great (a) hurry! How many fine horses! How many fine asses! Few books. How many pens? Little hope. So much dust! So much mud! So many times.

Baseness, *bassezza;* crime, *delitto;* traitor, *traditore;* cook, *cuoco;* hurry, *fretta;* book, *libro;* pen, *penna;* hope, *speranza;* dust, *polve;* mud, *fango;* time, *volta.*

How many times! As many times. Several times. Several days. What pride! (how much). What misery! (how much).

Several, *parecchio;* day, *giorno;* pride, *orgoglio;* misery, *miseria.*

VI.—COMPARATIVES AND SUPERLATIVES.

1. Comparison of superiority and inferiority.

Example.

voi siete più *ricco di me,*   you are *richer than* I.

io sono meno *ricco* di *voi*,	I am *less* rich *than* you.
vostra sorella è più *saggia* della *mia*,	your sister is *wiser than* mine.
vostra sorella è meglio *vestita* della *mia*,	your sister is *better* dressed *than* mine.
Lucia è peggio *educata* di *Maria*,	Lucy is brought up *worse than* Mary.
più *bianca* della *neve*,	*whiter than* snow.
più *ricco* di *Creso*,	*richer than* Crœsus.

(The English conjunction *than* is generally translated by *di*, or its compounds *del, dello, della, dei, degli, delle*, when the comparison is between nouns or pronouns.)

Example.

è meglio *tardi* che *mai*,	it is *better* late *than* never.
meglio *morire* che *cedere*,	*better* die *than* yield.
piuttosto *vezzosa* che *bella*,	*rather* pretty *than* beautiful.
meno *male assolvere il reo* che *punir l' innocente*,	there is *less* harm in saving the guilty *than* in punishing the innocent.

(*Than* is translated by *che* when the comparison takes place between verbs, adverbs, adjectives, or sentences.)

Example.

più *bella* di quel che *mai fosse*,	*handsomer than* she ever was.
spende più di quello che *guadagna*, *spende* più che non *guadagna*,	he spends *more than* he earns.

(The above forms are peculiar to the Italian.)

2. Comparatives of equality.

Example.

ella è tanto *modesta* quanto *è bella*, così *modesta* come *bella*, *modesta* sì com' *essa è bella*, *modesta* quanto *bella*,	she is *as* modest *as* she is beautiful.
schietto come *l' oro*,	pure *as* gold.

COMPARATIVES AND SUPERLATIVES.   25

bianca come *la neve,*	*as* white *as* snow.
voi avete tanto *danaro* quanto *ne ho io,*	you have *as* much money *as* I have.
avete tanti *amici* quanti *ne ho io,*	you have *as* many friends *as* I have.
avete quanto *danaro vi abbisogna,*	you have *as* much money *as* you need.
troverete amici quanti *ne volete,*	you'll find *as* many friends *as* you wish.
quanto più *studia* tanto meno *impara,* più *studia* meno *impara,*	*the more* he studies *the less* he learns.

3. The relative superlative is made by adding the article to the comparative of superiority.

Example.

il più *eloquente oratore* del *secolo,*	*the most* eloquent orator *of* the age.
il più *destro spadaccino* d' *Italia,*	*the most* skilful swordsman *in* Italy.

(In many cases, as in the last example, the English preposition *in* is translated *di* in Italian.)

4. The absolute superlative is made by translating *very* into *assai* or *molto.*

Ex.   *uomo* assai *dotto,*   a *very* learned man.
      è molto *bella,*   she is *very* beautiful.

or else by changing the termination of the adjective into *issimo,* in a few cases of adjectives in *re,* into *errimo.*

Example.

*Uomo dott-*issimo, *very* learned man, from *dotto.*
*Donna bell-*issima, *very* beautiful woman, from *bello* fem. *bella.*
*Consigliere sav-*issimo, *very* wise counsellor, from *savio.*
*Principe ricch-*issimo, *very* rich prince, from *ricco.*
*Versi dolc-*issimi, *very* sweet verses, from *dolce,* pl. *dolci.*
*Illustr-*issimo *Signore, most* illustrious Sir, from *illustre.*
*Poeta celeb-*errimo, *very* celebrated poet, from *celebre.*

D

(a) The adjectives that take *errimo* instead of *issimo* in the superlative, are all derived from a Latin in *er*,—as *celebre, salubre, acre*, &c.

5. There are some forms of comparative and superlative derived from the Latin, of very frequent occurrence.

maggiore,	greater.	*massimo,*	greatest.
minore,	less.	*minimo,*	least.
migliore,	better.	*ottimo,*	best.
peggiore,	worse.	*pessimo,*	worst.
superiore,	higher.	*supremo* or *sommo,*	highest.
inferiore,	lower.	*infimo* or *imo,*	lowest.
esteriore,	outward.	*estremo,*	outmost.
interiore,	inward.	*intimo,*	inmost.

(a) *Migliore* and *peggiore*, adjectives, must not be confounded with *meglio* and *peggio*, adverbs: these latter may be used as substantives:—*Le donne non iscelgono sempre* il meglio, women do not always choose *the best*.

Exercise.

The mother seems younger than the daughter. The daughter is less handsome than the mother. The son is taller than the father. The father is less rich than the son. Mary is wiser than Lucy—wiser than you.

Mother, *madre;* daughter, *figlia;* young, *giovine;* handsome, *bello;* son, *figlio;* rich, *ricco;* tall, *grande;* father, *padre;* Mary, *Maria;* wise, *saggio;* Lucy, *Lucia;* you, *voi;* seems, *pare;* is, *è.*

You are as wise as your sister. Your sister is as silly as your mother. She is as silly as she is handsome. The brother is as rich as the sister. The sister is richer than the brother. She is as good as she is fair.

Sister, *sorella;* silly, *sciocco;* brother, *fratello;* good, *buono;* your, *vostro,* fem. *vostra;* you are, *siete;* she, *ella.*

He is rather learned than witty. She is rather infirm than aged. He is rather rash than brave. He is brave as a lion. She is as white as snow. Whiter than snow. Braver than a lion. Silent as the grave.

COMPARATIVES AND SUPERLATIVES.

Learned, *dotto;* witty, *ingegnoso;* infirm, *infermo;* aged, *attempato;* rash, *temerario;* brave, *valoroso;* brave, *ardito;* lion, *leone;* white, *bianco;* snow, *neve;* silent, *muto;* grave, *tomba.*

Better to-day than to-morrow. Man is stronger than woman. Better an egg to-day than a hen to-morrow. Better weep with the righteous than exult with the iniquitous. Better perish once than always tremble. Death sooner than disgrace.

To-day, *oggi;* to-morrow, *domani;* man, *uomo;* woman, *donna;* strong, *forte;* egg, *uovo;* hen, *gallina;* to weep, *piangere;* righteous, *giusto* (pl.); to exult, *esultare;* iniquitous, *iniquo* (pl.); to perish, *perire;* once, *una volta;* to tremble, *tremare;* always, *sempre;* death, *morte;* disgrace, *disonore.*

The Arabian horses are better than the English. The earth is larger than the moon. The usurer is worse than the thief. Virtue is the highest happiness. No worse enemy than a faithless friend. The white horse is the best.

Arabian horse, *cavallo Arabo;* English, *Inglese;* earth, *terra;* moon, *luna;* usurer, *usuraio;* thief, *ladro;* virtue, *virtù;* happiness, *bene;* no worse, *nessun peggiore;* enemy, *nemico;* friend, *amico;* faithless, *infido.*

She is very handsome. He is very wise. The English climate is very healthy. England is the freest country in the world. He is the most profound philosopher of the age. The most profound thinker in Germany. The greatest talker.

Handsome, *bello;* wise, *saggio;* English climate, *clima Inglese;* healthy, *salubre;* England, *Inghilterra;* country, *paese;* free, *libero;* world, *mondo;* profound, *profondo;* philosopher, *filosofo;* age, *secolo;* thinker, *pensatore;* Germany, *Germania;* talker, *ciarlone.*

Your most humble servant. A very pretty girl. With

the greatest pleasure. With the least trouble. A man of [an] excellent (best) heart. Two most beautiful horses. Very accomplished gentlemen. Very profound scholars. The finest horse.

Servant, *servo;* humble, *umile;* girl, *ragazza;* pretty, *vezzoso;* pleasure, *piacere;* trouble, *disturbo;* heart, *cuore;* gentleman, *signore;* accomplished, *compito;* scholar, *letterato;* fine, beautiful, *bello.*

VII.—AUGMENTATIVES AND DIMINUTIVES.

1. Italian nouns, adjectives, and sometimes even adverbs, receive some modifications known under the appellation of *augmentatives* and *diminutives.*

These are extremely arbitrary, both as to forms and meanings, sometimes also about genders: they are not amenable to positive rules, and should be used sparingly.

The following examples comprehend the most common and regular forms:—

Examples.

Libro, book: *librone,* large book; *libraccio,* great ugly book; *libretto, libricino,* little book; *libercolo, libricciatolo,* worthless book, pamphlet.

Uomo, man; *ometto,* mannikin; *omicciatolo,* contemptible little man.

Donna, woman; *donnone* (masc.), large woman; *donnetta, donnicciuola,* little woman, gossiping woman; *donnaccia,* bad woman.

Casa, house; *casone* (masc.), big house; *casaccia,* great ugly house; *casetta, casuccia, casino* (masc.), little house, cottage; *casipola,* small ricketty house.

Camera, room; *camerino* (masc.), *cameretta, cameraccia,* little room.

AUGMENTATIVES AND DIMINUTIVES.

Strada, street or road; *strad*one (masc.), wide road; *strad*accia, bad road; *strad*etta, *strad*icciuola, lane, path, alley.

Uccello, bird; *uccell*ino, *uccell*etto, *uccell*uccio, *uccell*inetto, pretty little bird.

Contadino, countryman; *contadin*ello, country lad; *contadin*otto, young, stout-built countryman.

Tavola, table; *tavol*ino (masc.), small table, card or writing table, side table.

Gente, people; *gent*ame (masc.), mob; *gent*aglia, rabble.

Bambino, infant; *bambin*ello. *Orto*, garden; *ort*icello.

Signore, *signora*, gentleman, lady; *signor*ino, *signor*ina.

Conte, count; *cont*ino. *Principe*, prince; *princip*ino.

Padrone, *padrona*, master, mistress; *padron*cino, *padron*cina.

Riso, laugh; *ris*olino, pretty laugh; *sorriso*, smile; *sorris*etto, sweet smile.

Bastone, stick; *baston*cello. *Capanna*, cottage; *capann*uccia.

Albero, tree; *arb*oscello, graceful young tree, shrub.

Fiore, flower; *fior*etto, *fior*ellino, floweret, sweet flower.

Bestia, animal; *besti*one (masc.), *besti*accia, great ugly beast; *besti*uola, *besti*olina, *besti*olino (masc.), graceful little animal.

Vento, wind; *vent*icello, light wind. *Aura*, breeze; *aur*etta, light breeze.

Vecchio, *vecchia*, old man, old woman; *vecchi*erello, *vecchi*erella, pleasant little old man or woman.

Pazzo, fool; *pazz*accio, disagreeable fool; *pazz*erello, pleasant fool.

Angelo, angel; *angiol*etto, *angiol*ino, dear angel.

Sciocco, fool, foolish; *sciocc*one, *sciocc*herello.

Grasso, stout; *grass*accio, fat; *grass*otto, *grass*occio, plump.

Tenero, soft; *tener*ello, very young and tender.

Grande, tall; *grand*icello. *Lungo*, long; *lungh*etto.

Caro, dear ; *car*ino. *Piccolo*, small ; *piccolett*o, tiny.
*Vis*ino *graziosett*o (from *viso grazioso*), charming little face.
*Navicell*a *piccolett*a (*nave piccola*), pretty tiny boat.
*Bambinett*o *tenere*llo (*bambino tenero*), very tender darling infant.
Rosso, red ; *rossi*ccio, ruddy ; *rossastro*, reddish.
Verde, green ; *verd*igno, *verd*astro, greenish.
Giallo, yellow ; *giallo*gnolo, yellowish.
Bruno, brown ; *brun*azzo, dingy brown.
Bene, well ; *ben*ino, pretty well ; *ben*one, quite well.

2. The use of the above forms, although conveying in themselves the augmentative or diminutive meaning, do not exclude additional adjectives to the same effect: we can say thus, without fear of redundance.

Example.

*mirate quel piccolo cagn*olino !   look at that dear little dog !
*che grazioso uccell*etto !   what a pretty, pretty bird !

Exercise.

The little-old-man resting on his little-stick. The young-peasant-girl, with her little-pet-lambs. This girl is a little-angel. What a pretty-little-face! Poor-little-creature ! dear little-bird ! sweet little-flower !

Old man, *vecchio ;* stick, *bastone ;* peasant girl, *contadina ;* lamb, *agnello ;* girl, *ragazza ;* angel, *angelo ;* face, *viso ;* pretty, *leggiadro ;* creature, *creatura ;* poor, *povero ;* bird, *uccello ;* flower, *fiore ;* dear, *caro ;* sweet, *dolce ;* resting on his, *appoggiato al suo ;* with her, *coi suoi.* This, *questa ;* what, *che.*

You have bought a house : a big-house. The prince has bought a palace : a low-strong-built-palace. A bad-old-hat. A large-ugly-book. You have done very well. Come rather quick. Read rather-slowly.

House, *casa ;* prince, *principe ;* palace, *palazzo,* (low-strong-built to be expressed by diminutive in *otto*); hat, *cappello ;* old, *vecchio ;* book, *libro ;* large, *grande ;* well, *bene ;* quick, *presto ;* slowly, *adagio ;* you have,

avete; has, *ha;* bought, *comprato;* you have done, *avete fatto;* come, *venite;* read, *leggete.*
You are a great-fool. She is a dear-little-fool. Stop a little-moment. Where have you bought that pretty-little-love-of-a-dog? A little-rivulet watered the sweet-little-meadows. See that nice-little-cottage. Where have you bought that great-ugly-horse?

Fool, *sciocco*, or *pazzo;* moment, *momento;* dog, *cane;* that, *quel;* rivulet, *ruscello;* pretty, *grazioso;* cottage, *capanna;* that, *quella;* meadow, *prato;* sweet, *dolce;* nice, *leggiadro;* you are, *siete;* she is, *è;* stop, *fermatevi;* where have you bought? *dove avete comprato?* watered, *bagnava;* see, *vedete.*

The breeze whispers among the boughs of the little-grove. Let us rest on the tender young-grass.

breeze, *aura;* bough, *ramo;* grove, *bosco;* grass, *erba;* tender, *tenera;* whispers, *susurra;* let us rest, *riposiamoci.*

VIII.—NUMERAL ADJECTIVES.

1. The cardinal numbers are :—

0, *zero*.	13, *tredici*.	80, *ottanta*.
1, *uno*.	14, *quattordici*.	90, *novanta*.
2, *due*.	15, *quindici*.	100, *cento*.
3, *tre*.	16, *sedici*.	200, *duecento* or
4, *quattro*.	17, *diciassette*.	*dugento*.
5, *cinque*.	18, *diciotto*.	300, *trecento*, etc.
6, *sei*.	19, *diciannove*.	1000, *mille*.
7, *sette*.	20, *venti*.	2000, *due mila*.
8, *otto*.	30, *trenta*.	3000, *tre mila*.
9, *nove*.	40, *quaranta*.	100,000, *cento mila*,
10, *dieci*.	50, *cinquanta*.	etc. etc.
11, *undici*.	60, *sessanta*.	1,000,000, *un milione*,
12, *dodici*.	70, *settanta*.	etc.

32 ITALIAN GRAMMAR.

2. Cardinal numbers are indeclinable.

(a) Except *uno*, feminine *una ;* as *uno scudo*, a crown; *una lira*, a pound; and *mille*, one thousand; *due mila*, two thousand; *dieci mila*, ten thousand, etc.; also, *milione*, pl. *milioni ; bilione*, etc.

(b) 21, 31, 41, 51, etc., are written *vent' uno, trent' uno*, etc., and the nouns united with them can be used either in the plural or the singular. Ex. *vent' uno scudo, vent' uno scudi*, or *scudi vent' uno*, twenty-one crowns.

3. The ordinal numbers are :—

1st *primo*.	11th *undecimo, undicesimo*, or *decimo primo*.
2nd *secondo*.	12th *duodecimo, dodicesimo*, or *decimo secondo*.
3rd *terzo*.	
4th *quarto*.	13th *tredicesimo*, or *decimo terzo*.
5th *quinto*.	14th *quattordicesimo*, or *decimo quarto*.
6th *sesto*.	15th *quindicesimo*, or *decimo quinto*, etc.
7th *settimo*.	20th *ventesimo*, or *vigesimo*.
8th *ottavo*.	21st *ventunesimo*, or *ventesimo primo*.
9th *nono*.	22nd *ventiduesimo*, or *ventesimo secondo*.
10th *decimo*.	etc.

100th *centesimo ;* 1000th *millesimo*, etc.

4. Ordinal numbers have four terminations like adjectives in *o*.

Ex. *il primo scudo,* the first crown.
la prima volta, the first time.
i primi studi, the first studies.
le prime lettere, the first letters.

5. Numeral substantives are :—

un mezzo, fem. *una mezza*, one-half.
la metà, the half, pl. *le due metà*, both halves.
un paio, pl. *le paia*, pair.
una decina, *le decine*, half-a-score or 10.
una dozzina, *le dozzine*, a dozen.
una ventina, *le ventine,* a score.

so *trentina, quarantina, cinquantina*, &c. a set of 30, 40, 50.

un centinaio, pl. *le centinaia*, a hundred.
un migliaio, *le migliaia*, a thousand.
un milione, *i milioni*, a million.
un bilione, *i bilioni*, a billion, etc.

NUMERAL ADJECTIVES. 33

6. The following peculiarities respecting numbers are of importance.

Examples:

L' *anno* mille ottocento cinquant' uno — never diciotto cento, etc.	the year *one thousand eight hundred*, or eighteen hundred, and fifty-one.
Tasso morì nel *mille cinque cento novanta cinque*, or nell' anno mille, etc.	Tasso died *in* fifteen hundred ninety-five, or *in the year*, etc.
quanti ne *abbiamo del mese?* ai quanti *siamo del mese?*	*what is the day* of the month?
oggi è il primo,	to-day is *the first*.
oggi è il dieci, ne *abbiamo* dieci,	to-day is *the tenth*.
Napoleone morì il cinque *Maggio, mille ottocento vent' uno*,	Napoleon died on *the fifth of* May, eighteen hundred twenty-one.
Londra, il 10 Marzo, or, ai 10 Marzo, or, li 10 Marzo,	London, March 10*th*.
che ora *è?*	what o'clock is it?
è l'una,	it is *one o'clock*.
sono le quattro,	it is *four o'clock*.
sono le dieci e mezza, *sono* le dieci e mezzo,	it is half-past ten.
mezzogiorno e un quarto,	a quarter-past twelve (at noon).
mezzogiorno e mezzo,	half-past twelve (at noon).
le sei meno un quarto,	a quarter to six.
le tre meno venti,	twenty minutes before three.
entro un' ora,	in an hour.
fra tre giorni,	within three days.
da oggi a otto,	this day a week.
da domani a quindici,	to-morrow a fortnight.
sei mesi fa,	six months ago.
da qui a sei mesi,	six months hence.
da sei mesi in qua,	for the last six months.

due via due fa quattro, twice two is four.
sei via sei trentasei, six times thirty-six.
Luigi Decimo Ottavo, Louis *the* Eighteenth.
libro primo : capitolo quinto, book *the* first, chapter *the* fifth.
gli autori del secolo decimo quarto,
gli autori del trecento, } the authors of the fourteenth century.
Tasso fioriva nel secolo decimo sesto,
or, *nel* cinquencento, } Tasso flourished in the sixteenth century.

Exercise.

Seven children. Four boys and three girls. A boy and a girl. Forty-one pounds. Six thousand combatants. Four thousand five hundred foot, and fifteen hundred horse. Washington died in seventeen hundred and ninety-nine.

Child, *figlio;* boy, *maschio;* girl, *femmina;* pound, *lira;* combatant, *combattente;* foot, *fanti;* horse, *cavalli;* died, *mori.*

Francis the First. Charles the Fifth. On the twenty-fourth of February. Petrarch flourished towards the middle of the fourteenth century. She died at five o'clock. The morning, at a quarter to eleven. It is half-past eleven. Galileo flourished in the sixteenth century.

Francis, *Francesco;* Charles, *Carlo;* February, *Febbraio;* towards, *verso;* Petrarch, *Petrarca;* middle, *metà;* fourteenth and sixteenth century (in two manners); morning, *mattina;* flourished, *fioriva.*

Tasso, canto thirteenth, stanza twenty-fourth. He returned with [a] few hundreds of men. He brought me [a] few dozens of gloves. Two pair of boots. He has lost several thousands of pounds. I am satisfied with one half. She died nine months ago.

Few, *poco,* adject., or *alcuno;* glove, *guanto;* boot, *stivale;* pound, *lira;* month, *mese;* several, *parecchio,* adject.; returned, *tornò;* he brought me, *mi portò;*

he has lost, *ha perduto;* I am satisfied with, *mi contento di.*
Come again in six weeks. This day a fortnight. Six weeks from this. For the last three weeks. Within nine months. Seven times seven is forty-nine. He comes within the year. He comes this day a week. He comes a month from this, or a month hence.

Year, *anno;* week, *settimana;* come again, *tornate;* he comes, *viene.*

IX.—PERSONAL PRONOUNS.

1. Personal pronouns are declined with prepositions.

Nom.	*io,*	I.	*noi,*	we.
Gen.	*di me,*	of me.	*di noi,*	of us.
Dat.	*a me,*	to me.	*a noi,*	to us.
Acc.	*me,*	me.	*noi,*	us.
Abl.	{ *da me,*	from me.	*da noi,*	from us.
	in me,	in me.	*in noi,*	in us.
	con me,	with me.	*con noi,*	with us.
	etc.		etc.	
Nom.	*tu,*	thou.	*voi,*	you.
Gen.	*di te,*	of thee.	*di voi,*	of you.
Dat.	*a te,*	to thee.	*a voi,*	to you.
Acc.	*te,*	thee.	*voi,*	you.
Abl.	*da te,*	from thee.	*da voi,*	from you.
	etc.		etc.	

No Nominative.
Gen. *di se,* of himself, of herself, of itself, of themselves.
Dat. *a se,* to himself, to herself, etc.
Acc. *se,* himself, herself, etc.
Abl. *da se,* from himself, etc.
etc.

(*a*) *I'* may be used instead of *io.*
(*b*) *Meco, teco, seco,* are used instead of *con me, con te, con se.*

Nom.	egli,	he.	eglino,	they, (mas.)
Gen.	di lui,	of him.	di loro,	of them.
Dat.	a lui,	to him.	a loro,	to them.
Acc.	lui,	him.	loro,	them.
Abl.	da lui, etc.	from him.	da loro, etc.	from them.
Nom.	ella,	she.	elleno,	they, (fem.)
Gen.	di lei,	of her.	di loro,	of them.
Dat.	a lei,	to her.	a loro,	to them.
Acc.	lei,	her.	loro,	them.
Abl.	da lei, etc.	from her.	da loro, etc.	from them.

(*a*) *Ei* or *E'* may be used instead of *egli* and *eglino*.

2. The nominative pronouns *io, noi, tu, voi, egli, eglino, ella, elleno,* may be, and are generally, omitted before the verbs.

    Ex. *Penso a' miei figli,*   I think of my children.
        Piange il marito,   She mourns for her husband.

(*a*) Except (i.) when they are required to distinguish the person of the verb.

    Ex. *s'* io avessi *danaro,*   if I had money.
        se tu avessi *pazienza,* if thou hadst patience.

(ii.)—To avoid ambiguity.

    Ex. *i due sposi tacquero alquanto:* the two betrothed were silent for
        alfine ella *parlò,*   a while, at length she spoke.

(iii.)—When a peculiar stress or emphasis is laid on the pronoun.

    Ex. *comando* io,   it is *I* who command.
       io *son che prego,* it is *I* who beg.
      lo strepito lo fate voi, it is *you* who make a row.

(iv.)—When two or more pronouns are placed in contrast or antithesis.

    Ex. *se non volete cantar* voi, if *you* do not wish to sing,
        canterò io,   *I* shall.

(v.)—Whenever the pronoun is required by taste or euphony.

Examples.

t' ama ella *tanto?*   does *she* love thee so much?
ti sei tu fatto schiavo or così? hast *thou* become so great a slave?

(*b*) In all cases the repetition of the same pronoun is to be avoided.

Ex. io *pranzo quando posso,*
pranzo quando io posso,
pranzo quando posso,
but never
io *pranzo quando io posso,*
} *I* dine when *I* can.

3. Besides their regular declension with prepositions, the pronouns have peculiar forms which are called *conjunctive* pronouns. These are :

Dat. & A. *mi*, (instead of *a me, me*) { to me, me, to myself, myself.

ti, „ (*a te, te*) { to thee, thee, to thyself, thyself.

ci, or *ne*, „ (*a noi, noi*) { to us, us, to ourselves, ourselves.

vi, „ (*a voi, voi*) { to you, you, to yourselves, yourselves.

si, „ (*a se, se*) { to himself, himself, to herself, herself, etc.

Dat. only. *gli*, „ (*a lui*) to him, to it, (dat. m. sg.)
le, „ (*a lei*) to her, to it, (dat. f. sing.)

Acc. only. *lo*, or *il*, „ (*lui*) him, it, (acc. mas. sing.)
la, „ (*lei*) her, it, (acc. fem. sing.)
gli, or *li*, „ (*loro*) them, (acc. mas. plur.)
le, „ (*loro*) them, (acc. fem. plur.)

Gen. *ne*, of him, of her, of them, of it, some, any, hence, (French *en*).

Dat. *ci*, or *vi*, to it, there, (French *y*.)

Dat. *loro*, to them, used without preposition, instead of *a loro*.

(*a*) The pronouns *lo, la, gli, le*, are subject to the same elisions as the same words as articles.

(*b*) The pronouns *mi, ti, si, vi, ne*, may also suffer elision before any vowel; *ci* only before *i*.

4. The conjunctive pronouns are sometimes placed after the verb and joined to it : sometimes placed before it.

Example.

ascoltate-mi *quando* vi *parlo*, listen *to me* when I speak *to you.*

(*a*) They are generally joined to the verb, after it;

(i.)—After the infinitive.
   Ex. *vorrei* parlar-vi, I wish to speak *to you*.
 (ii.)—After the infinitive present.
   Ex. vedendo-lo, seeing *him*.
     avendo-lo *veduto*, having seen *him*.
(iii.)—After the participle past, when used without an auxiliary.
  Ex. veduto-lo (*i. e. avendolo veduto*), having seen *him*.
(iv.)—After the 2nd person sing. and the 1st and 2nd plur. of the imperative when used affirmatively.
   Ex. parla-gli, speak (thou) *to him*.
     parliamo-gli, let us speak *to him*.
     parlate-gli, speak (you) *to him*.
 (*b*) In all other moods and tenses; in the 3rd person sing. and plur. of the imperative, and in the whole of the imperative *when used negatively*, the pronoun is *usually*, though *not necessarily*, placed before the verb.

       Examples.
egli mi *ascolta quando io* gli *parlo*, he listens *to me* when I speak *to him*.
la *vedete?*   do you see *her?*
non mi *parlate*,   do not speak *to me*.
non ne *parliamo*,   let us not talk *about it*.
mi *risponda quando io* lo *inter-* let him answer *me* when I question
 rogo,   him.

 (*c*) The junction of the pronoun with the verb may give rise to
 (i.)—The suppression of the last vowel or syllable of the verb, especially in the infinitive.
       Examples.
non voglio veder-lo (vedere-lo), I do not wish to *see him*.
non posso scior-lo (sciorre-lo), I cannot *untie it*.
 (ii.)—To some reduplication of the consonant of the pronoun, when the verb terminates with an accented vowel.
       Examples.
dimmi il vero (di'-mi),   tell *me* the truth.
diemmela (me-la-die' *or* die'-me-la), he gave *it to me*.

 5. The conjunctive pronoun *is*, and *must be*, *generally*, preferred to the regular declension.
 (*d*) Unless,—(i.)—a peculiar stress is laid upon the pronoun.
   Ex. *parlo* a voi, it is *to you* I speak.
 (ii.)—Two or more pronouns are dependent on the same verb, especially if they be placed in contrast or antithesis.
       Examples.
parlo a lui *e* a lei,   I speak *to him* and *to her*.
parlo a lui *non* a lei,   I speak *to him* not *to her*.

chiamo lui *e non* lei,   I call *him* not *her*.
noi *inviteremo* loro *quando eglino*⎫
  avranno invitato noi,   ⎬ *we* shall invite *them* when *they*
Gl' *inviteremo quando ci avranno*⎪ shall have invited *us*.
  invitati,   ⎭

6. The conjunctive pronouns *mi, ti, ci, vi, si*, change their *i* into *e*, before *lo, la, gli, le, ne*.

  Ex. ve la *presento* (vi-la),   I introduce *her to you*.
      te lo *concedo* (ti-lo),   I grant *it to thee*.
      me ne *parlaste* (mi-ne),   you spoke *of it to me*.

7. The conjunctive pronouns *gli* (to him), and *le* (to her), are both changed into *glie* before *lo, la, li, le, ne*.

Examples.

gliene *parlo* {gli-ne,}   I speak *to him of it*.
          {le-ne,}   I speak *to her of it*.
glieli *raccomando* {gli-li,}   I recommend *them* (m.) to him.
               {le-li,}   I recommend *them* (m.) to her.
gliele *raccomando* {gli-le,}   I recommend *them* (f.) *to him*.
               {le-le,}   I recommend *them* (f.) *to her*.

(*a*) In all these junctions of pronouns,

(i.)—The first person takes precedence of the second, the second of the third.

Examples.

egli mi ti *raccomanda*,   he recommends *thee to me (to me thee)*.
io te lo *raccomando*,   I recommend *him to thee (to thee him)*.

(ii.)—The dative takes precedence of the accusative.

  Ex. glielo *raccomando*,   I recommend *him to her (to her him)*.
       gliela *raccomando*,   I recommend *her to him (to him her)*.

8. Attention should be paid to the following forms of pronouns added to the reflected verbs.

Mi *vanto*, I boast (*myself*); me ne *vanto*, I boast (*myself*) *of it*.

Ti *penti*, thou repentest (*thyself*); te ne *penti*, thou repentest (*thyself of it*).

Si *lagna*, he complains (*himself*); se ne *lagna*, he complains (*himself of it*).

Ci *lusinghiamo*, we flatter (*ourselves*); ce ne *lusinghiamo*, we flatter (*ourselves of it*).

Vi *dolete*, you complain (*yourselves*) ; ve ne *dolete*, you complain (yourselves of it).

Si *lodano*, they praise *themselves;* se ne *lodano*, they praise (themselves for it).

*Non posso vantar*mi, I cannot boast (*myself*).

*Non vuol pentir*si, he will not repent (*himself*).

*Non avete ragione di vantar*vene, you have no reason to boast (*yourselves of it*).

*Vantat*i, boast (*thyself*) ; *vantat*ene, boast (*thyself of it*).

Si *vanti*, let him boast (*himself*) ; se ne *vanti*, let him boast (*himself of it*).

*Vantiamo*ci, let us boast (*ourselves*) ; *non ci vantiamo*, let us not boast (*ourselves*).

*Vantate*vene, boast (*yourselves of it*) ; *non ve ne vantate*, do not boast (*yourselves of it*).

Mi *avvezzo*, I accustom *myself;* mi ci *avvezzo*, I accustom (*myself to it*).

Ti *avvezzi*, thou accustomest *thyself;* ti ci *avvezzi*, etc.

Si *avvezza*, he accustoms *himself;* ci si *avvezza*, etc.

Ci *avvezziamo*, we accustom *ourselves;* vi ci *avvezziamo*, etc.

Vi *avvezzate*, you accustom *yourselves ;* vi ci *avvezzate*, etc.

Si *avvezzano*, they accustom *themselves;* ci si *avvezzano*, etc.

Si *avvezzino*, let them accustom *themselves*.

Ci si *avvezzino*, let them accustom *themselves to it*.

Non ci si *avvezzino*, let them not accustom *themselves to it*.

*Avvezziamo*vici, let us accustom *ourselves to it*.

Non ci *avvezziamo*, let us not accustom *ourselves*.

*Avezzate*vici, accustom *yourselves to it*.

Non vi ci *avvezzate*, do not accustom yourselves to it.

*Non posso avvezzar*mi, I cannot accustom *myself*.

*Non posso avvezzar*mici, I cannot accustom *myself to it*.

Non mi *posso avvezzare*, I cannot accustom *myself*.

Non mi ci *posso avvezzare*, I cannot accustom myself to it.

*Dovete avvezzar*vi,
Vi *dovete avvezzare*, } you must accustom *yourselves*.

PERSONAL PRONOUNS.

*Dovreste avvezzar*vici, } you ought to accustom *your*-
Vi ci *dovreste avvezzare,* }   *selves to it.*

Exercise.

She weeps. Does she weep? He rides. I walk. I walk and he rides. I come with thee. Go with her. Breakfast with us. Dine with me. He always speaks of himself. You shall not have it from me. Do not put your trust in her. She always speaks of herself.

Weeps, or does weep, *piange;* rides, *va a cavallo;* walk, *vo a piedi;* come, *vengo;* go, *andate;* breakfast, *fate colazione;* dine, *pranzate;* always speaks, *parla sempre;* shall not have it, *non l' avrete;* do not put your trust, *non abbiate fede.*

Speak to me. Speak to him. Speak to me, not to him. Do you speak *to me?* Do you speak to me, or to him? Speak to her. Speak to her about (of) it. Do not speak to me about it. Speak to us. Speak to us about it.

Speak, or do speak, *parlate;* do not speak, *non parlate.*

I esteem him. I esteem her. I esteem him and her. I see you. You see me. You see me, but I do not see you. Do you see the tower? I see it. Do you see the castle? I see it. Do you see me? Do you see her? Do you see us? Do you see him?

Tower, *torre;* castle, *castello;* I esteem, *stimo;* I see, *vedo;* you see, or do you see? *vedete.*

I had two sons. I have lost them. I had two daughters. I have married them. I will punish you. I will punish you for (of) it. I will punish him. God will punish her. God will punish us. Do not punish me. Do not punish us. Punish him and not her.

Son, *figlio;* daughter, *figlia;* God, *Dio;* I had, *aveva;* I have lost, *ho perduti;* I have married, *ho maritate;* I will punish, *punirò;* will punish, *punirà;* punish, *punite;* do not punish, *non punite.*

Do you see those trees? I see them. I do not see

hem. I cannot see them. Do you see those houses? I do'nt see them. I do not see any (of them). Do you see any ship? I do not see any (of them). Have you many children? I have none (not any of them).

Those trees, *quegli alberi;* those houses, *quelle case;* any ship, *alcuna nave;* many children, *molti figli;* do you see, *vedete?* I see, *vedo;* I do not see, *non vedo;* I cannot see, *non posso vedere;* I do not see any of them, turn, I not of them see any; any, *alcuna;* have you, *avete?* I have, *ho.* I have none, turn, *I not of them have any;* any, *alcuno.*

Bring (to) me the book. Give (to) her the pen. Will you have the book? Take it. Will you have the pen? Ask for it, but do not take it. Will you have the book and the pen? Take them. Do you see the gentlemen? I see them. Do you see the ladies? I see them. Do you see the ladies and the gentlemen? I see them. Do you see the lady? I see her. Do you see the lady and the gentleman? I see them.

book, *libro;* pen, *penna;* gentleman, *signore;* lady, *signora;* give, *date;* bring, *portate;* will you have, *volete?* take, *prendete;* ask for, *domandate;* do not take, *non prendete.*

This is the book. Do you wish it? Ask it? Ask me for it. Ask it of me. Ask it of me, not of any one else. Seeing us he called us. Seeing her he loved her. Having seen her he hated her. Having met you I spoke to you.

This is, *ecco;* do you wish, *volete?* ask, *domandate;* ask me for it, ask it of me, turn, *ask to me it;* any one else, *alcun altro;* seeing, *vedendo;* he called, *chiamò;* he loved, *amò;* having seen, *avendo veduto,* or *veduto,* he hated, *odiò;* having met, *avendo incontrati;* I spoke, *parlai.*

Do you want the book? Here it is. I have seen him. I have seen him, but not you. I have seen him alone.

PERSONAL PRONOUNS. 43

I have seen you both. Do you see those gentlemen? There they are. Do you see those ladies? There they are!

Do you want, *volete?* here is! there is! here are! there are! *ecco!* (the pronoun is always added to this word, after it;) I have seen, *ho veduto;* but, *ma;* alone, *solo;* both, *entrambi;* those, *quei*, fem. *quelle.*

He recommends us. He recommends us to you. He recommends me to thee. He recommends you to me. I command it. I command it to you. I recommend her to you. Speak [you] to her. Speak to her of it. Do [you] not speak to her of it. Show [you] it. Show it to me. Do not show it to me.

Recommends, *raccomanda;* command, *comando;* I recommend, *raccomando;* speak, *parlate;* show, *mostrate;* do not show, *non mostrate.*

Have you a watch? Show it to him. Have you a purse? Show it to her. Have you a book? Will you show it to me? I will show it to you. I will show it to you, but not to her. Is this your wife? Introduce me to her. Introduce her to me.

Watch, *oriuolo;* purse, *borsa;* your wife, *vostra moglie;* have you, *avete?* will you show, *volete mostrare?* I will show, *mostrerò;* is this, *è questa?* introduce, *presentate.*

Where is your wife? There she is. I will introduce you to her, but not to her sister. I will introduce her to you, but not her sister.

Where is? *dov' è?* I will introduce, *presenterò;* sister, *sorella.*

I speak to you. I speak to thee. I speak to thee of it. Answer (to) me. She answers (to) me. She will not answer (to) me. I will not answer (to) you. I will not answer (to) her. Answer (to) him. Answer (to) her. Do not answer (to) her.

I speak, *parlo;* answer [thou,] *rispondi;* she answers,

risponde; she will not answer, *non vuol rispondere;* I will not answer, *non voglio rispondere,* or *non risponderò;* answer [you], *rispondete;* do not answer [you,] *non rispondete.*

Give (to) me. Give it. Give it to me. Give me the book. Tell (to) me the truth. Tell (to) her, what I told (to) thee. Speak to me about (of) it. Tell [thou] (to) me thy opinion about (of) it. Tell [you] (to) me your opinion about it. Tell it to me.

Give [thou,] *dà;* tell [thou,] *di;* truth, *vero;* what I told, *ciò che dissi;* speak, *parla;* thy opinion, *il tuo parere;* tell [you], *dite;* your opinion, *il vostro parere.*

Give (to) her the book. Give (to) him the book. Do not give him the book. Do not give it to her. Do not give it to her but to him. Give us some wine. Give me some bread. Give me some. Give her some. Give some to him also.

Give [thou], *dà;* give [you], *date;* do not give [thou], *non dare;* do not give [you], *non date;* wine, *vino;* bread, *pane;* some, turn, *of it;* to him also, turn, *also to him;* also, *anche.*

Have you some bread? Give us some. Hast thou some nuts? Give us some. Have you a newspaper? Give it to him. Hast thou an apple? Give it to her. Have you many horses? Give us one. Hast thou many pens? Give us one.

nuts, *noci;* newspaper, *giornale;* apple, *mela;* many horses, *molti cavalli; give us one,* turn, *give us of them one;* one, *uno;* many pens, *molte penne;* one, *una.*

I consent to it. I cannot consent to it. Have you some paper? I have not any. Will you have some? I do not want any. Think of (to) it. I think of it. I must think of it. Do not think of it. Let us think of it. Let them think of it. Let us not think of it.

I consent, *acconsento;* I cannot consent, *non posso acconsentire;* paper, *carta;* I have not, *non ho;* any,

PERSONAL PRONOUNS. 45

turn, *of it;* will you have, *volete? some,* turn, *of it;* I do not want, *non voglio;* think *of it,* turn, *think to it;* think [thou], *pensa;* think [you], *pensate;* I think, *penso;* I must think, *debbo pensare;* do not think [you], *non pensate;* let us think, *pensiamo;* let them think, *pensino.*

She esteems him. He esteems her. He esteems her, but she does not esteem him. They invited us. We must invite them. We will invite her. We will invite her and him. Invite her if she invites you.

Esteems, *stima;* does not esteem, *non istima;* they invited, *invitarono;* we must invite, *dobbiamo invitare;* we will invite, *inviteremo;* invite, *invitate;* she invites, *invita.*

I complain (myself). I complain of it. I dare not complain of it. She repents (herself) of it. She will not repent. We do not repent (ourselves) of it. Let us repent (ourselves). Let us not repent (ourselves) of it.

I complain, *lagno;* dare complain, *oso lagnare;* she repents, *pente;* will not repent, *non vuol pentire;* we do not repent, *non pentiamo;* let us repent, *pentiamo;* let us not repent, *non pentiamo,* (reflective verbs throughout).

Repent (thyself). Repent (yourselves). Let them repent (themselves). I force myself. I force myself to it. You cannot force me to it. Do not force me to it. She forces herself. Do not force him. Do not force him to it. Do not force us to it.

Repent, *penti,* plur. *pentite;* let them repent, *pentano;* I force, *sforzo;* you cannot force, *non potete sforzare;* do not force, *non forzate;* she forces, *sforza.*

X.—POSSESSIVE PRONOUNS.

1. Possessive Pronouns are used with articles.

il mio,	la mia,	i miei,	le mie,	my, mine.
il tuo,	la tua,	i tuoi,	le tue,	thy, thine.
il suo,	la sua,	i suoi,	le sue,	his, her, hers, its.
il nostro,	la nostra,	i nostri,	le nostre,	our, ours.
il vostro,	la vostra,	i vostri,	le vostre,	your, yours.
il loro,	la loro,	i loro,	le loro,	their, theirs.

(*a*) *Loro* is merely the personal pronoun *di loro* (of them) used without preposition.

2. The article is generally omitted when these pronouns are added to nouns of kindred or dignity in the singular.

Example.

parlatene a vostro zio,	speak of it to your uncle.
l' ho dato a mia cugina,	I have given it to my cousin.
fu presentata a Sua Maestà,	she was introduced to His Majesty.
obbligatissimo a vostra eccellenza,	much obliged to your Excellency.

3. The article is, however, used even with such nouns.

  I. In the plural number.

Example.

l' ho dato alle *mie cugine*,   I have given it to my cousins.

  II. When the noun precedes the pronoun.

Example.

obbligatissimo all' *Eccellenza vostra*,   much obliged to your Excellency.

  III. Or when an adjective occurs between the pronoun and the noun.

Example.

l' ho dato alla *mia cara cugina*,   I have given it to my dear cousin.

  IV. The pronoun *loro* invariably bears the article.

Example.

il loro padre è in villa,   their father is in the country.

POSSESSIVE PRONOUNS.

(*b*) The article is omitted when the pronoun is added to a noun, taken in an indefinite, partitive, or limited sense.

Example.

quel cavallo è mio,	{ That horse is mine—that is, belongs to me, one of my horses.
quel cavallo è il mio,	{ That is *my* horse—that is, *the* horse that belongs to me.
questi sono miei figli,	{ These are *my* children—that is, *some* of my children.
questi sono i miei figli,	{ These are *my* children—that is, *all my* children, or *those* of my children you know of, or allusion has been made *to*.

(*c*) The following examples deserve particular attention.

l' ho dato ad un mio amico,	I have given it to a friend *of mine.*
non è mio amico,	he is *no* friend *of mine.*
fate a modo mio,	do (after *my own* way) as I tell you.
vostro danno,	{ (*your own* loss or injury), so much the worse for you.
È colpa vostra,	it is *your own* fault.
casa mia è casa vostra,	{ my house is (*your own*) at your service.
sono in pena per causa vostra,	I am distressed on *your* account.
fatelo con vostro comodo,	do it at *your own* convenience.
vado io in sua vece,	I go in *his* stead.
l' avvenire non è in nostra mano,	the future is not in *our* hand.
l' ho scritto di propria mano,	I have written it with *my own* hand.
con vostra licenza,	by *your* leave.
sentite, amico mio,	hear me, *my dear* friend.
che discorsi son questi, Signor mio?	how do you speak, Sir?

4. The same possessive pronouns are both adjectives and substantive, that is, they may be used with or without the noun.

Example.

datemi il vostro libro e prendete il mio,	give me *your* book and take *mine.*
tutto quel che vedete è vostro,	all that you see is *your own.*

5. The possessive pronoun should be omitted whenever it may be obviously implied.

Example.

piange il marito,	{ she mourns for (the) *her* husband.

ha perduto la testa,	he has lost (the head) *his* senses.
piego il ginocchio,	I bend (the) *my* knee.
portami il cappello,	bring me (the) *my* hat.

6. The personal pronoun is often substituted to the possessive.

Example.

levati il cappello,	take off *thy* hat, (to thyself, the hat.)
gli han mozzo il capo,	they have cut *his* head off, (to him, the.)
mi cadde ai piedi,	he fell at *my* feet, (to me, at the.)
s' è rotto un braccio,	he broke *his* arm, (to himself, an.)
non ti son rivale,	I am not *thy* rival, (to thee a.)

Exercise.

Here is my horse and there is yours. Where is your brother? Where are your brothers? Who is your cousin? Who are your cousins? Tell it to your father-in-law. Tell it to your brothers-in-law.

Horse, *cavallo*; brother, *fratello*; cousin, *cugino*, fem. *cugina*; father-in-law, *suocero*, fem. *suocera*; brother-in-law, *cognato*, fem. *cognata*; here is, and there is, *ecco, ed ecco*; where is, *dov' è?* where are, *dove sono?* who is, *chi è?* who are, *chi sono?* tell, *dite*.

Call your mother-in-law. Speak to your sister-in-law. Call your sisters-in-law. What is your ladyship's pleasure? His Holiness is in Rome. Your uncle has married my younger sister. Your pretty sister will be married to-morrow.

Call, *chiamate*; speak, *parlate*; what is the pleasure of, *che comanda?* has married, *ha sposato*; will be married, *si sposerà*; Ladyship, *Signoria*; Holiness, *Santità*; uncle, *zio*; younger sister, *sorella minore*; pretty, *bella*; sister, *sorellina*; to-morrow, *domani*.

DEMONSTRATIVE PRONOUNS.

This is my horse. Will you buy my horses? This horse is mine. This is my niece. This is my nephew. This is my best horse. This is my beloved niece. He is my friend. He is no friend of mine.

This, *questo,* fem. *questa;* nephew, niece, *nipote;* beloved, *diletto;* friend, *amico;* will you buy, *volete comprare?* is, *è.*

These are thy nieces. These are his nephews. These are their children. These are his sons. These are her daughters. Remember, he is thy son. Remember, they are thy children. Remember, I am thy wife.

These, *questi,* fem. *queste;* child, *figlio;* son, *figlio;* daughter, *figlia;* wife, *moglie;* are, *sono;* remember, *ricordati che;* he is, *è;* I am, *sono.*

She has lost her parents. Their father is dead. They have stolen his purse. He has cut his finger. His Majesty has lost his crown. This is his Lordship's horse. They throw themselves at your Lordship's feet. They throw themselves at your feet.

Parent, *genitore;* purse, *borsa;* finger, *dito;* Majesty, *Maestà;* crown, *corona;* lordship, *signoria;* foot, *piede;* has lost, *ha perduto;* dead, *morto;* has cut, *s' è tagliate;* have stolen, *hanno rubato;* they throw themselves, *si gettano.*

XI.—DEMONSTRATIVE PRONOUNS.

1. Demonstrative Pronouns are used with prepositions.

questo,	*questa,*	*questi,*	*queste,*	this.
cotesto,	*cotesta,*	*cotesti,*	*coteste,*	that.
quello,	*quella,*	*quelli,*	*quelle,*	

(*a*) *Quello, quel,* in the singular, *quegli, quei,* or *que'* in the plural, follow the same euphonic rules as the articles *dello, del, degli, dei,* or *de'.*

Examples. quello *spirito*, pl. quegli *spiriti.*
quell' *ingegno*, quegl' *ingegni.*
quel *padre*, quei *padri.*

Quelli is only used when it stands alone without nouns.
Ex. in questi *campi e in* quelli, in *these* fields and *those.*

2. *Cotesto* and *quello* are both used for *that ;* but *cotesto* refers to the person spoken to, *quello* to the person or thing spoken of.

Example.

prendete questo *libro e portatemi* cotesto, take *this* book and bring me *that,* (*i. e.* the one near you.)

andatemi a prender quel *libro,* { go and fetch me *that* book, (*i. e.* the book yonder, away from you.

This rule is however often disregarded, and the two pronouns indiscriminately used one for the other.

3. *Questo* and *quello* are often contrasted in the sense of " the former," " the latter."

Example.

ondeggio fra la speranza e il timore, quella *mi sorride, e m' inganna,* questo *mi agghiaccia e mi uccide,* I waver betwixt hope and fear, *the one* smiles and allures me, *the other* chills and disheartens me.

4. Demonstrative pronouns may be used substantively or absolutely; that is, they may be referred to a noun either understood or implied.

Example.

questo *è il mio duolo,* *this* is my sorrow.
più sacra insegna è questa, *this* is a holier standard.
queste *son, vili, le battaglie vostre,* *these* are, ye cowards, your battles.

The following are used for persons only.

questi,
costui, } this man; *costei,* this woman; *costoro,* { these men.
these women.

quegli,
colui, } that man; *colei,* that woman; *coloro,* { those men.
those women.

Example.

è questi *il vostro Re*,   *this* is your King.
quegli *che vince*,   *he* who conquers.

(*b*) *Costui, costei, costoro, colui, colei, coloro,* often convey a meaning of contempt.

che vuol costui?   what does *this fellow* want?

Sometimes they are used in the sense of the highest admiration in poetry:—

"*Chi vuol veder quantunque può natura
E 'l ciel tra noi venga a mirar costei.*"
"Whoever would see all that Nature and Heaven
Can achieve here below, must come and behold *this one.*"

5. *Questo* and *quello* are used substantively for "this thing," "that thing," more commonly *ciò* for both.

Example.

chi ha fatto questo?   who has done *this?*
che significa ciò?   what is the meaning of *that?*

6. The English substantive pronoun *what,* i. e. "*that which,*" or "*all that which,*" must be resolved in Italian into *quello* or *ciò,* followed by the relative *che.*

Example.

fate quello che *vi piace,*
fate quel che *vi piace,*   } do *what* you please.
fate ciò che *vi piace,*

tutto ciò ch' *io m' abbia è tuo,*   *all* I have is thine.

questo è tutto ciò che *m' ha
detto,*   } this is *all* he told me.
ciò è quanto *mi ha detto,*

Exercise.

What is the name of this town? Who are these children? What are these papers? Do not speak to those children. That horse is lame. Those horses are lame. That glass is broken. Those glasses are broken.

Town, *paese;* child, *fanciullo;* paper, *carta;* glass, *specchio;* lame, *zoppo;* broken, *rotto;* what is the name of, *come si chiama?* who are, *chi sono?* what are, *che sono?* do not speak, *non parlate;* is, *è;* are, *sono.*

What are you doing in this town? What are you doing in that town? What is your son doing in that town? Bring me that picture. Fetch me that picture. Bring me those pictures. Take away this picture. Take away these pictures. Fetch me those pictures. Take away those pictures.

Town, *città;* picture, *quadro;* what are you doing, *che fate?* what is — doing, *che fa?* bring, *portate;* fetch, *andate a prendere;* take away, *portate via.*

This man is my best friend. That woman is my worst enemy. I can bear neither the husband nor the wife. That one is proud. This one is silly. My enemies laugh at me. My friends pity me. I do not know whether these or those anger me most.

Friend, *amico,* fem. *amica;* enemy, *nemico,* fem. *nemica;* husband, *marito;* wife, *moglie;* proud, *superbo;* silly, *sciocco;* is, *è;* I can bear, *non posso soffrire;* neither, nor, *nè, ne;* laugh at, *deridono;* pity, *compiangono;* I know not, *non so;* whether, *se,* or *o;* anger me most, *più m' irritano.*

(These or those at the end of the sentence.)

Choose between fortune and virtue. That one can make thee rich. This one alone happy. Who said this? Who has done that? Do what I bid. Believe all he says. Do not believe what that fellow says.

Fortune, *fortuna;* virtue, *virtù;* rich, *ricco;* happy, *felice;* alone, *solo;* choose, *scegli;* can make, *può fare;* who said, *chi disse?* who has done, *chi ha fatto?* do, *fate;* I bid, *comando;* believe, *credete;* he says, *dice;* do not believe, *non credete.*

He has bought these fields. He has sold those fields. He has bought these fields and sold those. Do not sell your field to that miser. Do not sell your fields to those misers. He buys those fields and sells these.

Field, *campo;* miser, *avaro;* he has bought, *ha comprato;* has sold, *ha venduto;* do not sell, *non vendete;* he buys, *compra;* sells, *vende.*

XII.—RELATIVE PRONOUNS.

1. *Quale,* who, which, that, as a Relative Pronoun, is generally declined with articles; adjectively and substantively.

Il quale, la quale, i quali, le quali, del quale, della quale, dei quali, delle quali, &c.

Example.

il qual *padre Cristoforo,*   *which* father Christopher.
l' uomo del quale *io parlo,*   the man *of whom* I speak.

2. *Che, cui, chi,* are more frequently employed. They are of all genders and numbers, and declined with prepositions only; they are used only substantively.

3. *Che* is used for all cases, but best in the nominative and accusative.

Ex.   *io che vi parlo,*   I *who* speak to you.
 il vino che bevete,   the wine you drink.
 l' uomo di ch' *io parlo,*   the man I speak *of.*

(*a*) The relative pronoun is not often omitted in Italian.

4. *Cui* is only used in the oblique cases, and best used in the genitive and ablative, with the prepositions *di, da, per, con, in,* &c.

Example.

l' uomo di cui *parlo,*   the man I speak *of.*
il padrone per cui *lavoro,*   the master I work *for.*

(*b*) *Cui* is never used in the nominative, nor often in the accusative; unless it be to avoid ambiguity.

Ex. *il muro cui nasconde la casa,*   the wall *which* the house hides.

Different from

il muro che nasconde la casa,   the wall *which* hides the house.

(*c*) *Cui* may be used without prepositions, instead of *di cui* in the sense of *whose*; and also instead of *a cui.*

Example.

l' eroe le cui gesta io canto,	the hero *whose* exploits I sing.
voi cui *fortuna ha posto in mano il freno,*	you *to whom* fortune entrusted the destinies, &c.

5. *Chi* is only used substantively for *he who, she who, they who, one who.*

Example.

chi *ama teme,*	he who loves fears.
guardatevi da chi *vi adula,*	beware of those who flatter you.
fidatevi di chi *vi vuol bene,*	trust one who loves you.

6. *Chi* is also used in the sense of *some*: this—that; one—another.

Example.

in questo mondo chi *sale* chi *scende,*	in this world *one* ascends, *another* falls.
chi *piangeva,* chi *rideva,*	{ *some* were crying, *some* laughing.

7. *Che* is also used substantively.

Example.

non abbiam che *mangiare,*	we have *nothing* to eat.
han di che *vivere,*	they have *wherewith* to live.
il che *è anche meglio,*	*which* is even better.
del che *io dubito,*	a thing *which* I doubt.

8. *Onde* is used instead of *di cui, da cui, con cui, per cui.*

Example.

l' anima gloriosa onde *si parla,*	} the glorious soul we speak *of.*
nella prigione ond' *ora è sciolta,*	in the prison she is now freed *from.*
il fuoco ond' *ardo,*	the fire I am burning *with.*
per quell' uscio ond' *era entrato,*	} the door he had come *through.*

9. *Quale, che, chi,* are also interrogative pronouns.

10. *Quale* means which? or what? and, as interrogative, is used without articles.

RELATIVE PRONOUNS.

Example.

qual *dei due volete?*	*which* of the two do you want?
di qual *giorno volete parlare?*	*what* day do you mean?
qual *uomo!*	*what* a man!
non so di quale *parliate,*	{ I do not know *of which* you speak.

11. *Chi* refers only to persons.

Example.

chi *è costei?*	*who* is this woman?
chi *sono costoro?*	*who* are these persons?
di chi *parlate?*	*who* are you speaking of?
a chi *pensate?*	*who* are you thinking of?
non so chi *sia,*	I know not *who* he may be.

12. *Che* means *what?* and is used both adjectively and substantively.

Example.

che *uomo!*	*what* a man!
che *uomo è?*	*what* sort of a man is he?
che *danari avete?*	{ *what* money have you? (how much money?)
che *volete?*	*what* do you want?
e tu, che *sei?*	and thou, *what* art thou?
a che *pensate?*	*what* are you thinking of?
non so che *cerchiate,*	{ I do not know *what* you may be looking for.

Exercise.

The man to whom you speak. The man who speaks to you. The horse I have bought. The money I have lent you. The friends who have forsaken us. The friends we have forsaken. The ladies you have invited.

You speak, *parlate;* speaks, *parla;* I have bought, *ho comprato;* I have lent, *ho prestato;* have forsaken, *hanno abbandonati;* we have forsaken, *abbiamo abbandonati;* you have invited, *avete invitate;* money, *danaro;* lady, *signora.*

The times in which we live. The letter I have read. The house we live in. The dangers from which we have escaped. The man who prides himself. The woman you hate. The house I come from. The girl you have seen.

We live, *viviamo;* I have read, *ho letta;* we live in, *abitiamo;* we have escaped, *siamo scampati;* prides, *gloria;* you hate, *odiate;* I come, *vengo;* you have seen, *avete veduta;* time, *tempo;* letter, *lettera;* danger, *pericolo;* girl, *fanciulla.*

The pens which I have mended. The friend I was living with. Who are you? What do you want? What are you speaking of? Who are you speaking of? Whom do you see? What do you see? Who wants me? What happened to you?

I have mended, *ho temperate;* I was living, *dimorava;* are you, *siete?* do you want, *volete?* are you speaking, *parlate?* do you see, *vedete?* wants, *vuole;* happened, *avvenne;* pen, *penna.*

What house is this? Which of these houses is yours? What [a] fine thing! What fools! How many fools? What will you give me? At what o'clock? Whose fault is it? How old are you? What are you laughing at? What day is it?

Thing, *cosa;* fine, *bello;* fool, *pazzo;* will you give, *volete dare?* what o'clock? (what hour?) hour, *ora;* whose fault is it? (of whom is the fault?) fault, *colpa;* how old are you? what age have you? age, *età;* have you, *avete?* what are you laughing at? (of what are you laughing?) are laughing, *ridete;* is it, *è?*

He who breathes hopes. Pity those who suffer. Have you nothing to do? I have nothing to hope. He has some one who deceives him. Blessed are those who weep. Who comes? What land is this? Which is your land?

Breathes, *spira;* hopes, *spera;* pity, *compiangete;* suffers, *soffre;* suffer, *soffrono;* have you nothing to do? (not have you what to do, or aught to do,) not have you, *non avete;* to do, *fare;* I have, *ho;* to hope, *sperare;* he has, *ha;* deceives, *inganna;* (some one who) one word; blessed, *beato*, pl. *beati*; weeps, *piange*; weep, *piangono*; comes, *viene*; land, *terra*.

XIII.—INDEFINITE PRONOUNS.

1. *Ogni*, every; *qualche*, some; *qualunque*, any, whatever, are adjective pronouns: they are of both genders, and only used in the singular.

Examples.

ogni *rosa ha le sue spine*,   *every* rose has its thorns.
manca da qualche *tempo*,   { he has been missing for *some* time.
mandami qualche *libro*,   send me *some* books.
fatelo in qualunque *modo*,   do it *any* way.

(*a*) *Qualsisia, qualsivoglia,* are synonymous with *qualunque.*

2. *Ognuno* (*ogni uno*), every one; *qualcuno* (*qualche uno*), some one, are substantive pronouns, and used in the singular only.

Example.

ognuno *lo dice*,   *every one* says so.
l' ho udito da qualcuno,   I have heard it from *somebody*.

(*b*) *Qualcheduno*, some one; *certuno*, a certain person; *taluno*, such a one, etc., are pronouns of the same nature.

3. *Alcuno*, some, any; *nessuno, niuno, veruno*, no one, none, not any, are used both adjectively and substantively; they are of two genders, and are also used in the plural.

Example.

se le trovate in alcun *luogo*,   if you find him *any* where.
ho comprato alcuni *libri*,   I have bought *a few* books.
qui non vi è alcuno,   *no one* is here.
non vi è nessuno,   there is *nobody*.
io non trovo nessun *rimedio*,   I find *no* remedy.
io non vi discernea veruna *cosa*,   I perceived *no* thing.
non lo dite a niuno,   tell it to *no one*.

(*c*) The Italian admits of a double negative.

4. *Tutto*, all, every, is of both genders and numbers, and is used both adjectively and substantively. It is generally followed by the article.

Example.

tutto il *mondo*,	*the whole* world.
tutti gli *uomini*,	*all* men.
io penso a tutto,	I think of *every thing*.
tutti *mi vogliono*,	*all* ask for me.

5. *Tale*, such; *medesimo, stesso*, same, &c., are mere adjectives, used in both genders and numbers, and declined with articles. Sometimes, however, they are used as substantive pronouns.

Example.

il tal *libro*,	*such a* book.
il medesimo *signore*,	*the same* gentleman.
tale *è la mia speranza*,	*such* is my hope.
è venuto quel tale,	*that certain person* is come.
non sono gli stessi.	they are not *the same*.

6. *Esso, essi; essa, esse*, it, are used sometimes as personal pronouns instead of *egli, eglino; ella, elleno*.

Desso, dessa, dessi, desse, are used in the sense of *the same*.

Ex. È desso, or *è quel desso*. It is *he*. It is *the same person*.

7. *Altro, altra, altri, altre*, other, is an adjective pronoun; but *altri, altrui*, are used substantively speaking of persons only; *altri*, in all cases; *altrui*, never in the nominative.

Example.

altri *è lieto*, altri *misero*, *one* is happy, *another* unhappy.
io non voglio la roba d'altri, } I do not wish *other people's*
io non voglio la roba altrui, } property.

fu apposto altrui, { It was laid *to the charge of other persons*.

8. The following examples may show other peculiarities respecting these pronouns.

INDEFINITE PRONOUNS.

Example.

non *vi è* alcuno *che sappia* tutto,	there is *no one* that knows *every thing*.
vi sfido tutti quanti,	I challenge you *as many as you are*.
tremo tutto quanto,	I tremble *all over*.
vengo di tutta fretta,	I come *in great haste*.
per quanti *sforzi facciate*,	*whatever* efforts you may make.
per *poter* che *egli abbia*,	*whatever* power he may have.
per quante *lagrime si spargano*,	*whatever* tears may be shed.
venne da me un certo tale,	*a certain man* called upon me.
certuni *s' imaginano*,	*certain people* fancy.
taluni *si lusingano*,	*some people* flatter themselves.
l' uno *si diverte*, l' altro *si dispera*,	*the one* makes fun, *the other* is in despair.
gli uni *e* gli altri *son mille*,	*both together* are a thousand.
ne diede a ciascun *d' essi*,	he gave some to *each* of them.
ne diede a ciascuna *di loro*,	
ciascheduno *lo vuole per se*.	*every one* wishes him for himself.
troverete qualcheduno,	you will find *somebody*.
chiunque *lo dice s' inganna*,	*whoever* says so is mistaken.
non cedo a chicchessia,	I yield to *no man in the world*.
mi arrendo a qualsisia *partito*,	I give in to *any* proposal.
non *cedo a* qualsivoglia *ragione*,	I yield to *no* reason.
non lo do per checchessia,	I do not give it for *any thing in the world*.
altri va, altri *viene*,	*some* go, *some* return.
altro *è il parlar di morte*, altro *è il morire*,	*one thing* it is to speak of death, *another* to die.
parliam d' altro,	let us speak of *something else*.
lo dico a te e non altrui,	I tell it thee and *no one else*.
non *desiderare la roba d'* altri,	do not covet *thy neighbour's* goods.
non *desiderare la roba* altrui,	
non *desiderare l'* altrui,	

sono arrivati ambedue, both are arrived.
ha perduto ambe *le braccia,* he has lost *both* arms.
Exercise.

Every moment. Every hour. Every man. Every woman. I do not fear any enemy. I do not fear any one. Somebody is at the door. Some friend is at the door. We have invited some friends for this evening. Some gentlemen and some ladies. Some of our relatives, and some of our friends.

moment, *momento;* hour, *ora;* enemy, *nemico;* door, *porta;* friend, *amico;* relative, *parente;* I do not fear, *non temo;* we have invited, *abbiamo invitato.*

I have some books. I have no books. I have given away all books. All my books. All women are angels. All are invited. I have lost every thing. I had many friends. I have lost them all. He had a large fortune; he has lost it all.

I have given away, *ho dati via;* are invited, *sono invitati;* I have lost, *ho perduto;* I had, *aveva;* I have lost, *ho perduti;* he had, *aveva;* he has lost, *ha perduta;* angel, *angelo;* fortune, *sostanza;* large, *grande.*

Whatever hope I had. I have no hope. Whatever reason you may have. Whatever reasons you may have. You have no reason. No man hates me. I owe no man anything. Do you see any one? I see no one. I find him no where. Some one wants you.

I had, *aveva;* I have no (I not have any) not have, *non ho;* you may have, *abbiate;* you have no (you not have any), not have, *non avete;* hates, *odia;* I owe no (I not owe to any), not owe, *non debbo;* do you see, *vedete?* I see, *vedo;* I find, *trovo;* find no where (not find in any place), place, *luogo;* wants, *domanda.*

The one is false, the other is credulous. Neither is to be trusted. Either the one or the other is wrong. Both are wrong. Neither is right. I know them both. I know them all. I know another. I know no one else. Somebody else will pay.

false, *bugiardo*; credulous, *credulo*; neither (neither the one nor the other), neither, nor, *nè—ne*; is to be trusted, *merita fede*; either, or, *o—o*; is wrong, *ha torto*; are wrong, *hanno torto*; is right, *ha ragione*; I know, *conosco*; I know another (of them I know another); I know no one else (not of them I know any other); somebody else (some other); will pay, *pagherà*.

XIV.—REGULAR VERBS.

1. There are three conjugations of regular verbs, the first in *are*, like *am-are*, to love; the second in *ere*, like *tem-ere*, to fear; the third in *ire*, like *dorm-ire*, to sleep.

(*a*) The conjugations ought to be four as in Latin; the second in ère long, as *tem-ère*; the third in ère short, as *créd-ère*, to believe; but as with the exception of the accent of the infinitive, the two conjugations are the same throughout, they are set down as one in most grammars.

2. In every Italian verb, distinction must be made between the *root*, that is, that part of the verb which remains unchanged as *am-*, *tem-*, *dorm-*, and the *termination* are, ere, ire, which changes for every mood, tense, number, and person.

3. The first vowel in the termination—*a* in the first conjugation, *e* in the second, *i* in the third, is called the characteristic; it constitutes the main difference between the conjugations, and runs more or less constantly throughout them; it is especially observable in the imperfect, indicative, and subjunctive, and in the preterit.

4. It is owing to this circumstance, that the above tenses, and the future and conditional are subject to less anomalies in the conjugation of irregular verbs, whereas

the greatest difficulties arise in the present, indicative, and subjunctive, in the imperative, and whenever the characteristic has been departed from in the regular conjugations.

The following paradigm of the three regular conjugations will enable the pupil to conjugate any regular verb, by applying the root of the verb in question to any of the desinences of the model verbs.

The accent has been laid upon the persons in which it falls upon the termination ; in all other cases it is to be understood to fall upon the root of the verb. Ex. *ám*-o, *am*-áva.

The accent however is never written, except at the end of the word, and is only given here as a direction to the learner.

1st—*am*-are, (to love.) 2nd—*tem*-ere, (to fear.)
3rd—*dorm*-ire, (to sleep.)

INDICATIVE MOOD.

PRESENT TENSE.

am-o— I love.	*tem*-o—I fear,	*dorm*-o—I sleep,
-i— thou lovest.	-i. &c.	-i. &c.
-a— he loves.	-e.	-e.
-iámo—we love.	-iámo.	-iámo.
-áte— ye love.	-éte.	-íte.
-ano—they love.	-ono.	-ono.

IMPERFECT.

am-áva— I was	*tem*-éva.	*dorm*-iva.
-ávi— loving	-évi.	-ívi.
-áva— or loved,	-éva.	-iva.
-avámo— &c.	-evámo.	-ivámo.
-ávate—	-eváte.	-iváte.
-ávano—	-évano.	-ívano.

REGULAR VERBS. 6

PRETERIT.

am-ái— I loved	tem-éi or étti.	dorm-ii.
-ásti— or did	-ésti.	-ísti.
-ò— love,	-è étte.	-ì.
-ámmo— &c.	-émmo.	-ímmo.
-áste—	-éste.	-íste.
-árono—	-érono—éttero.	-írono.

FUTURE.

am-erò— I shall	tem-erò.	dorm-irò.
-erái— or will	-erái.	-irái.
-erà— love,	-erà.	-irà.
-erémo— &c.	-erémo.	-irémo.
-eréte—	-eréte.	-iréte.
-eránno—	-eránno.	-iránno.

CONDITIONAL.

am-eréi—I should	tem-eréi.	dorm-iréi.
-erésti— or	-erésti.	-irésti.
-erébbe—would	-erébbe.	-irébbe.
-erémmo—love,	-erémmo.	-irémmo.
-eréste— &c.	-eréste.	-iréste.
-erébbero—	-erébbero.	-irébbero.

IMPERATIVE.

(No first person singular.)

am-a— love (thou).	tem-i.	dorm-i.
-i— let him love.	-a.	-a.
-iámo—let us love.	-iámo.	-iámo.
-áte— love (ye).	-éte.	-íte.
-ino—let them love	-ano.	-ano.

SUBJUNCTIVE MOOD.

PRESENT TENSE.

Che	That		
am-i—	I love	tem-a.	dorm-a.
-i—	or may	-a.	-a.
-i—	love,	-a.	-a.
-iámo—	&c.	-iámo.	-iámo.
-iáte—		-iáte.	-iáte.
-ino—		-ano.	-ano.

IMPERFECT.

Se	If		
am-ássi—	I loved	tem-éssi.	dorm-issi.
-ássi—	or	-éssi.	-íssi.
-asse—	might	-ésse.	-isse.
-ássimo—	love,	-éssimo.	-issimo.
-áste—	&c.	-éste.	-iste.
-ássero—		-éssero.	-íssero.

INFINITIVE MOOD.

PRESENT TENSE.

am-áre, to love.   tem-ére, to fear.   dorm-íre, to sleep.

PARTICIPLE PRESENT.

am-ánte, loving.   tem-énte, fearing.   dorm-énte, sleeping.

GERUND.

am-ándo, loving.   tem-éndo, fearing.   dorm-éndo, sleeping.

PARTICIPLE PAST.

am-áto, loved.   tem-úto, feared.   dorm-íto, slept.

(*b*) The participle present in *ante, ente*, is found only in a few verbs. It is therefore omitted in many grammars, which give the name of participle present to the gerund in *ando, endo*.

(*c*) To the second person singular of the imperative, the infinitive must be substituted after a negative. Ex. *Non temere*, do not fear. *Nè credere*, nor do thou believe.

REGULAR VERBS.

Exercise.

I love my friends. He fears the enemy. What dost thou fear? What do you fear? She sleeps. Do they sleep all night? Fear (thou) God and fear nothing else. They love me as I love them. They were sleeping. How long will she sleep? How long did she sleep? She would sleep still.

The English auxiliary *do* is omitted in the Italian; fear nothing else, turn (not fear any thing else); how long, *quanto tempo;* still, *ancora.*

You praise me. We praise you. You will blame him. They will blame her. She sings well. She will sing if you beg (pr. ind.) her. She always sang (imperf.) when I begged (imp.) her. They were sleeping (imp.) when you entered (pret.) We were singing when you called (pret.) us.

To praise, *lodare;* to blame, *biasimare;* to sing, *cantare;* to beg, *pregare;* to enter, *entrare;* to call, *chiamare;* always, *sempre;* when, *quando.*

I shall sing if you dance (pr. ind.) I would dance if you sang (sub. imp.) They will laugh if you sigh. They slept (imp.) while you talked (imp.) They will return without you. They would return before you. When do you return? When will you return? Return to-morrow.

To dance, *ballare;* to laugh, *ridere;* to sigh, *sospirare;* to talk, *parlare;* to return, *tornare;* without, *senza di;* before, *prima di;* to-morrow, *domani.*

Sing (thou) me the songs of thy country. Sing (you) me the songs of your country. Let him laugh if he dare (ind. pr.) Let him not lose his time. Do not lose thy time. Do not lose your time. Let him sleep if he thinks (pr. ind.) himself safe. Let them sleep if they think (pr. ind.) themselves safe.

To dare, *osare;* to lose, *perdere;* to think, *credere;* song, *canzone;* country, *patria;* safe, *sicuro;* time, *tempo.*

I would not fear him if all his friends fought (subj. imp.)

by his side. I would defend you, if a thousand enemies assailed (subj. imp.) you. They would pass their time agreeably if they studied (subj. imp.) [in] the morning and played (subj. imp.) [in] the evening. You would esteem her more if you knew (sub. imp.) her better.

To fight, *combattere;* to defend, *difendere;* to assail, *assalire;* to pass, *passare;* to study, *studiare;* to play, *giuocare;* to esteem, *stimare;* to know, *conoscere;* by his side, (at his side,) side, *fianco;* agreeably, *piacevolmente.*

Fearing him, she shunned (imp.) him. Seeing her, he talked (pret.) to her. He wishes rather to be feared than loved. Surrounded by the enemies he was still fighting (imp.)

To shun, *sfuggire;* he wishes rather to be, *vuol piuttosto essere;* to surround, *circondare;* still, *tuttavia.*

XV.—AUXILIARY VERBS.

1. The Auxiliary Verbs are *avere*, to have; *essere*, to be.

Pr. In.	Ho—I have,	Pr. In.	Sóno—I am.
	hái. etc.		séi.
	ha.		è.
	abbiámo.		siámo.
	avéte.		siéte.
	hánno.		sóno.
Imper.	*avéva*—I had.	Imper.	éra—I was.
	avévi.		éri.
	avéva.		éra.
	avevámo.		eravàmo.
	aveváte.		eravàte.
	avévano.		érano.

AUXILIARY VERBS.

Pret.	ébbi—I had.		Pret.	fúi—I was.
	avésti.			fósti.
	ébbe.			fu.
	avémmo.			fúmmo.
	avéste.			fóste.
	ébbero.			fúrono.
Fut.	avrò—I shall have.		Fut.	sarò—I shall be.
	avrái.			sarái.
	avrà.			sarà.
	avrémo.			sarémo.
	avréte.			saréte.
	avránno.			saránno.
Condit.	avréi—I should		Condit.	saréi—I should be
	avrésti. have.			sarésti.
	avrébbe.			sarébbe.
	avrémmo.			sarémmo.
	avréste.			saréste.
	avrébbero.			sarébbero.
Impera.	ábbi—have (thou).		Impera.	síi—be (thou)
	ábbia.			sía.
	abbiámo.			siámo.
	abbiáte.			siáte.
	ábbiano.			síano.
Sub. Pr.	ábbia—I may have.		Sub. Pr.	sía—I may be.
	ábbia.			sía.
	ábbia.			sía.
	abbiámo.			siámo.
	abbiáte.			siáte.
	ábbiano.			síano.
Imperf.	avéssi—I might		Imperf.	fóssi—I might be
	avéssi. have.			fóssi.
	avésse.			fósse.
	avéssimo.			fóssimo.
	avéste.			fóste.
	avéssero.			fóssero.
Infin.	avére—to have.		Infin.	éssere—to be.

Ger. *avéndo*—having.   Ger. *esséndo*—being.
Part. Past. } *avúto*—had.   Part. Past. } *státo*—been.

2. All compound tenses are formed analogously to the English. Only *essere* is, in its compound tenses, conjugated by itself.

Example.

ho avuto, I have had.   sono *stato,* I have been.
hanno avuto, they have had.   sono *stati,* they have been.
avremo avuto, we shall have had.   saremo *stati,* we shall have been.
avendo avuto, having had.   essendo *stato,* having been.

3. *Avere* is used for the compound tenses of active and neuter-active verbs.

Ex. *ho imparato,*   I have learnt.
avete dormito,   you have slept.
avevamo ceduto,   we had yielded.
ebbero vivuto,   they had lived.

4. *Essere* is used with passive, neuter-passive, and reflected verbs.

Ex. *sono lodato,*   I am praised.
sono stato lodato,   I have been praised.
ella era andata,   she had gone.
mi sono *lusingato,*   I have flattered myself.
ella si era *lusingata,*   she had flattered herself.

5. The participle past after *essere* must agree with the nominative.

Ex. *egli è stato lodato,*   *eglino sono stati lodati.*
ella è stata lodata,   *elleno sono state lodate.*

6. The participle past after *avere,* may or may not agree with the accusative.

Ex. *ha perduto il padre,*   he has lost his father.
ha perduto *ha perduta* } *la madre,*   he has lost his mother.
ha perduto *ha perduti* } *i genitori,*   he has lost his parents.

AUXILIARY VERBS.

7. It must, however, agree with the accusative when this precedes it.

Ex. *il padre che ha perduto,* the father whom he has lost.
la madre che ha perduta, the mother whom he has lost.
i genitori che ha perduti, the parents whom he has lost.

(*a*) The same rules apply to reflective verbs, when they have the force of active or transitive verbs.

Ex. *non mi son mai sognato una cosa simile,*
or, *non mi son mai sognata una cosa simile,*
but, *una cosa simile non mela son mai sognata,*
} I have never dreamt such a thing.

8. The verbs *andare, stare, venire,* are sometimes used as auxiliaries with the participle present.

Ex. *che* andate *cercando?* what *are* you seeking?
stavamo *giocando,* we *were* playing.
mi venne *punzecchiando,* he *was* teazing me.

9. *Venire* is also frequently used instead of *essere* with passive verbs.

Example.

venne *indotto ad andarsene,* he *was* persuaded to go away.
vengono *tratti in carcere,* they *are* dragged into prison.

10. The active verb assumes a passive meaning when preceded by the particle *si,* one, they, people.

(*a*) The particle *si* does not exactly correspond to the French *on,* or to the German *man,* to which it bears resemblance. The verb that follows the *si,* in Italian, must generally agree with the noun, which is, in fact, its nominative.

Example.

si loda *la povertà e* si amano *le ricchezze,* men praise poverty and love riches.

(In French, on loue la pauvreté, et on aime les richesses.)

The real meaning of the Italian is, " Poverty is praised and riches " are loved."

11. The following examples will give some useful hints as to the use of the particle *si.*

si vendono cavalli, horses are sold.
si è venduto un cavallo, a horse has been sold,
qui si parla Italiano, Italian is spoken here.
non si dicono queste cose, such things should not be said.

se ne parla dappertutto,	it is talked of everywhere.
si sogna ciò che si desidera,	one dreams what one wishes.
queste cose si sanno da tutti,	these things are known to all.
non se ne sa niente,	nothing is known about it.
non si può negarlo,	one cannot deny it.
si richiede coraggio per farlo,	it requires courage to do it.

Exercise.

I am hungry. You are thirsty. We were warm and they were cold. He was in a hurry. You shall be sleepy. If you were (imp. subj.) right I should be wrong. They were both right. My friend is wrong. You are wise. Why art thou in so great a hurry? How cold she is.

Hunger, *fame*; thirst, *sete*; warmth, *caldo*; cold, *freddo*; hurry, *fretta*; sleep, *sonno*; right, *ragione*; wrong, *torto*; why, *perchè*; so great, *tanto*; to be hungry, thirsty, warm, cold, &c., *aver fame, sete, etc.*; to be in a hurry, *aver fretta*; to be wise, *aver giudizio*; to be right, *aver ragione*; to be wrong, *aver torto*; how cold she is! what cold she has!

Be wise, my son. I have bought those books. These are the books (which) I have bought. This is the pen he has mended. The pens have been mended. I have mended the pens. You will have patience. Have patience. She will have courage. Let them have courage.

To buy, *comprare*; to mend, *temperare*; patience, *pazienza*; courage, *coraggio*; pen, *penna*.

Let her have patience. Let us be merciful. Let us forgive. You would be sure of success if you had (subj. imp.) patience. You will be forgiven if you (pr. ind.) ask for pardon. You shall have friends if you are not (pr. subj.) so fickle. They would be rich if they had (subj. imp.) all they had, (imp. ind.)

Merciful, *misericordioso*; to forgive, *perdonare*; sure, *certo*; of success, *di riuscire*; you will be forgiven (to you will be forgiven); to ask for, *domandare*;

AUXILIARY VERBS. 71

pardon, *perdono;* fickle, *volubile;* rich, *ricco;* all they had (all that which they had).

The country would be armed if it had (subj. imp.) any fear of war. The enemies will be beaten if they have (pr. ind.) the courage to assail us. Have (thou) mercy. Be (you) just if you wish (pr. ind.) to be free. Let them have life and liberty. Be this the last proof of my kindness. Be friends.

To arm, *armare;* to beat, *battere;* to assail, *assalire;* to wish, *volere;* country, *paese;* fear, *timore;* war, *guerra;* enemy, *nemico;* courage, *coraggio;* mercy, *pietà;* life, *vita;* liberty, *libertà;* last, *ultimo;* proof, *prova;* kindness, *bontà*.

Provided thou hast learned. Whoever he may be I do not fear him. Whatever power he may have. I would try if I were (subj. imp.) sure of success. Although he might have been deceived. Whenever he may repent (himself). Wherever he may be apprehended.

Provided, *purchè;* whoever, *chiunque;* whatever, *qualunque;* although, *quantunque;* whenever, *ogniqualvolta;* wherever, *ovunque;* (all these pronouns and conjunctions must be followed by the subjunctive.)

To learn, *imparare;* to deceive, *ingannare;* to try, *tentare;* to repent, *pentirsi;* to apprehend, *arrestare;* power, *potere*.

I have deceived him. He has deceived himself. They would have deceived themselves. They talk of war. These birds are found in the mountains. People did not believe the news. These wonders are seen every day. French is spoken here. Horses are sold cheaper in winter than in summer,

To deceive, *ingannare;* to talk or speak, *parlare;* to find, *trovare;* to believe, *credere;* to see, *vedere;* to sell, *vendere;* bird, *uccello;* mountain, *monte;* news, *nuova;* wonder, *prodigio;* French, *Francese;* cheap, *a buon mercato;* winter, *inverno;* summer, *estate*.

Friendship is strengthened by time. Children are spoilt by too much kindness. Men are bought and sold like cattle. It required more patience.

To strengthen, *raffermare*; to spoil, *guastare*; to require, *richiedere*; friendship, *amicizia*; time, *tempo*; kindness, *bontà*; cattle, *bestiame*.

XVI.—MOODS AND TENSES.

1. The Italian has two past tenses, the Preterit or Perfect, and the Imperfect tense.

2. The Preterit expresses a complete and definite action.

Example.

gli parlai *ieri*, I *spoke* to him yesterday.
l' aspettai *gran tempo*, I *waited* for him a long time.

3. The Imperfect expresses an incomplete, or an indefinitely continued or repeated action: also an action dependent upon another equally past action.

Example.

io l' aspettava *ancora*, I *was waiting* for him yet.

io gliene parlava *un giorno*, { I *was speaking* to him of it one day.

ella dormiva *quando entrai*, { she *was sleeping* when I entered.

cavalcava *quand' era giovine*, { I *rode* (*used to ride*) when I was young.

gli parlava *ogni volta che l' incontrava*, { I *spoke* (*used to speak*) to him whenever I *met* (*chanced to meet*) him.

4. The following examples illustrate the use of these tenses:—

presso i Romani si ardevano i cadaveri, dead bodies *were burnt* among the Romans.

MOODS AND TENSES.

così si scriveva *nei tempi andati*,	thus *did* men *write* in olden times.
così si scriveva *mentre fioriva il* buon gusto,	thus *did* men *write* when good taste *prevailed*.
così si scrisse *finché* fiori *il buon gusto*,	thus *did* men *write* so long as good taste *prevailed*.
vidi *un naviglio su cui* erano *due donne che* piangevano,	I *saw* a ship on which *were* two women *weeping*.
c'era *una volta un Re*,	{ once upon a time there *was* a King.
fu *già un Re il cui nome* era ——	a King *was* once whose name *was* ——
fu *coronato quand'* era *ancora fanciullo*,	he *was* crowned whilst he *was* yet a child.
era *già re mentre* era *ancora fanciullo*,	he *was* already a king, whilst yet a child.
io era *innocente e pur* fui *punito*,	I *was* innocent, and yet *was* punished.
invitò *quanti amici aveva*,	{ he *invited* as many friends as he *had*.
morì *il giorno stesso in cui io* nacqui.	he *died* on the very day I *was born*.
spuntava *il giorno quand' egli* morì,	day *was dawning* when he *died*.

(*a*) These tenses are almost invariably subject to the same rules as in French, only the Italian admits of greater freedom and latitude; and the tenses are indiscriminately substituted to one another.

5. The compound of the present expresses a past action belonging to a period either not entirely elapsed or recent.

Example.

gli ho parlato *oggi stesso*,	{ I *have spoken* to him this very day.
me ne ha parlato *ieri*,	{ he *has spoken* to me about it yesterday.

(*b*) In the second of these examples the Preterit may be equally used,— *me ne* parlò *ieri*.

H

6. The compound of the Imperfect expresses a past action, anterior to another past action.

Example.

l' avea veduto *prima ch' egli* I *had* seen him ere he en-
entrasse, tered.

7. The compound of the Preterit is used in the same sense, but after the conjunctions, *quando,* when ; *poichè,* since ; *tosto che,* as soon as, etc.

Example.

quando l' ebbi *veduto,*
tosto ch' io l' ebbi *veduto,*
appena io l' ebbi *veduto,*
veduto che l' ebbi,

lo chiamai.

when I *had* seen him,
as soon as I *saw* him,
hardly *did* I see him,

I called out to him.

8. Any verb preceded by another verb, either expressed or understood, implying desire, wish, fear, doubt, belief, or command, is generally used in the Subjunctive.

Example.

io non so chi tu sia,	I know not who thou *art.*
si dice ch' egli sia *morto,*	they say he *is* dead.
credeva che fosse *partito,*	I thought he *had* gone.
vorrei che tu mi credessi,	I would wish thee to *believe* me.
pensate quanto ciò mi affliggesse,	think how much this *distressed* me.
lo farò quando vi piaccia,	I will do it whenever it *may please* you.
ditegli che parta *quando vuole,*	tell him he *may go* when he likes.
basta ch' io sappia *dove andate,*	enough that I *know* where you go.

(*c*) The whole theory of the Subjunctive depends on this,—that a verb expressing an action upon which any doubt falls, should be used in the Subjunctive.

Example.

si dà per certo *che la pace* they say for certain that the
sia *fatta,* peace *is* made.

MOODS AND TENSES.

è certo *che la pace* è *fatta*,	it is positive that the peace *is* made.
voglio sposare una donna che m' ama,	I wish to marry a woman who *loves* me.
voglio sposare una donna che m' ami,	I will marry some woman who *may love* me.
è il miglior amico ch' io ho,	he is the best friend I *have*.
è il miglior amico ch' io m' abbia,	he is the best friend (perhaps) that I *have*.
se lo vedete *parlategliene*,	if you *see* him speak to him about it.
gliene parlerò se lo vedo,	I shall speak to him about it if I *see* him.
gliene parlerei se lo vedessi,	I would speak to him about it if I *saw* him.
m' *avrebbe ucciso se tu non* eri,	he would have killed me, if it *had* not been for thee.
credo *ch' egli* viva *ancora*,	*I think* he *lives* still.
credo *che il Redentor mio* vive,	*I believe* that my Redeemer *lives*.

9. The following examples are given as an illustration of the use of the infinitive.

1st. The infinitive without preposition.

vorrei parlarvi,	I wish *to* speak to you.
quanto vorrei non saper scrivere,	how I would wish not *to* know *how to* write.
io non poteva crederlo,	I could not believe it.
l' ho fatto venire,	I have made him come.
lasciatela piangere,	let her weep.
bisogna aver fede,	one must have faith.
dovete rispettarlo,	you must respect him.
basta guardarla,	it is enough *to* look at her.

2nd. The infinitive with the preposition *di*.

spero di *vedervi*,	I hope *to* see you.
vi prego di *spiegarvi meglio*,	I beg you *to* explain yourself better.

gli ho promesso di *pagarlo*,	I have promised *to* pay him.
è contenta di *sposarlo*,	she is willing *to* marry him.
mi comanda di *aspettarlo*,	he bids me wait for him.
è risoluto di *morire*,	he is determined *to* die.

3rd. The infinitive with the preposition *a*.

comincio a *capire*,	I begin *to* understand.
impariamo a *cantare*,	we learn *to* sing.
vi consiglio a *star zitto*,	I advise you *to* hold your tongue.
son pronto a *riceverlo*,	I am ready *to* receive him.
son solito ad *alzarmi per tempo*,	I am used *to* rise betimes.
non mi forzate a *rispondervi*,	do not force me *to* answer you.
disponetevi a *morire*,	prepare yourself *to* die.
avvezzatevi a *soffrire*,	accustom yourself *to* endure.

4th. The infinitive with *di* or *a*.

persuadetelo di, *or* ad *andarsene*,	induce him *to* go.
pregatela di, *or* a *restare*,	beg her *to* stay.

5th. The infinitive with *per*.

vengo per *dirvi*,	I come *to (in order to)* tell you.
lo dice per *farmi dispetto*,	he says it *to (in order to)* spite me.
lo fo' per *compiacervi*,	I do it *in order to* please you.

6th. The infinitive with *da*.

ho da *scrivere una lettera*,	I have a letter *to* write.
sono cose da *non credersi*,	they are things not *to* be believed.
è uomo da *farlo*,	he is the man *to* do it.

7th. The infinitive with the article.

mi piace il *cavalcare*,	I like riding.
stanco del tanto viaggiare,	tired *of* so much travelling.
siate cauti nello *scrivere*,	be cautious *in* writing.
lo conosco al *vestire*,	I know him *by* his dress.
è virtù il *parlar poco*,	*to* talk little is a virtue.
non lo stogliete dal rompersi il collo,	do not prevent him *from* breaking his neck.

10. The gerund is never used with a preposition or article, the infinitive being usually substituted.

Example.

insegnando s' *impara*,
coll' insegnare *s' impara*, } one learns *by teaching*.

l' appetito viene mangiando,
l' appetito viene nel mangiare, } appetite comes *by eating*.

11. The participle present in *ante, ente*, is seldom used; the relative pronoun with the indicative being generally substituted.

Example.

diversi principii tendenti *allo stesso scopo, or* che tendono *allo stesso scopo,* } different principles *tending to the same aim*.

selvaggi viventi *di carne umana, or* che vivono *di carne umana,* } savages *living* on human flesh.

Exercise.

Whilst she sang I heard a noise. She was talking and I listened. I listened all the time that she sang. I believed it because you assured me of it. He related it to me when they called him and took him away. It rained and I had no umbrella.

To hear, *sentire;* to listen, *ascoltare;* to believe, *credere,* to assure, *assicurare;* to relate, *raccontare;* to call, *chiamare;* to take, *menare;* away, *via;* to rain, *piovere;* it rains, *piove;* whilst, *mentre;* noise, *romore;* all the time that, *tutto il tempo che;* because, *perchè;* when, *quando;* umbrella, *ombrella;* I had no (I not had).

The army was returning from France when the King called together a council. In ancient times the greatest men ploughed. He heard that they were slaves. Alexander treated his enemies humanely. Alexander treated Porus as a King.

To return, *tornare;* to call together, *convocare;* to plough, *arare la terra;* to hear, *udire;* to treat, *trattare;* army, *esercito;* council, *concilio;* ancient, *antico;* time, *tempo;* slave, *schiavo;* Alexander, *Alessandro;* Porus, *Poro;* humanely, *umanamente;* as a King, *da Re.*

As many as were in that house were arrested. He was yet young when he was raised to the throne. The war lasted thirty years. The war raged still when the King died. In the time that the French were driven from Italy. At that time the French were still in Italy.

To arrest, *arrestare;* to raise, *innalzare;* to last, *durare;* to rage, *infierire;* to die, *morire;* to drive, *cacciare;* as many as, *quanti;* throne, *trono;* war, *guerra;* yet, still, *ancora;* in the time that, *al tempo che;* French, *Francese.*

I think it rains. I see it rains. I thought you had spoken to him. I was sure you had spoken to him. I am certain she loves him. I believe for certain she loves him. Do you fancy I am a fool? Tell me where you go. Do you know where you go?

To think or believe, *credere;* to see, *vedere;* to fancy, *imaginarsi;* tell me, *ditemi;* do you know, *sapete?* sure, *certo;* for certain, *di certo;* where, *dove;* a fool, *pazzo.*

I had seen your danger before you fell (subj. imp.) into it. When I had seen the danger I avoided it. If you had seen the danger you would have avoided it. As soon as they had received the order they obeyed. If they had received the letter they would have answered. When I receive a letter I answer.

To fall, *cadere;* to avoid, *evitare;* to receive, *ricevere;* to obey, *ubbidire;* to answer, *riscontrare;* danger, *pericolo;* before, *prima che;* into it, *vi;* order, *ordine;* as soon as, *tosto che.*

They have suffered him to die. I was not able to prevent it. It suffices that you ask it. They request you to forgive (to) him. They wish to embrace them. They are content to forget the past. They order me to set out instantly. They asked to pay.

To suffer, *lasciare;* to die, *morire:* to be able, *potere;* to prevent, *impedire;* it suffices, *basta;* to ask, *domandare;* (it suffices to you to ask it, or it suffices that you ask it;) to request, *supplicare;* to forgive, *perdonare;* to wish, *desiderare;* to embrace, *abbracciare;* to be content, *contentarsi;* to forget, *dimenticare;* to order, *comandare;* to set out, *partire;* to pay, *pagare;* they asked, (they wished;) the past, *il passato;* instantly, *subito.*

I demand to be heard. I advise you to listen to me. They exhorted me to have patience. The trees begin to blossom. I have learnt to hold my tongue. Are you ready to fight? Do not force me to punish you. He speaks so to insult me. They jest to make you laugh. I lend you a book to read.

To demand, *domandare;* to hear or listen to, *ascoltare;* to exhort, *esortare;* to begin, *cominciare;* to blossom, *germogliare;* to learn, *imparare;* to hold one's tongue, *tacersi;* to fight, *battersi;* to force, *sforzare;* to punish, *punire;* to insult, *insultare;* to jest, *scherzare;* to make, *fare;* to laugh, *ridere;* to lend, *prestare;* to read, *leggere;* tree, *albero;* ready, *pronto;* so, *cosi.*

It is necessary to be cautious. It is not enough to have money. The greatest victory is to conquer one's self. The best way to obtain honours is not always to deserve them. Lavish in spending other people's money. Unequalled in painting.

To be necessary, *bisognare;* to be enough, *bastare;* to conquer, *vincere;* to obtain, *conseguire;* to spend, *spendere;* to paint, *dipingere;* to deserve, *meritare;* cautious, *cauto;* money, *danaro;* victory, *vittoria;* way, *modo;* honour, *onore;* lavish, *prodigo;* other people's money, (other's) one word, *altri;* unequalled, *senza pari.*

He earns his living by teaching. He was drowned (drowned himself) in crossing the river. Mortals, ever wavering between hope and fear. I hear a woman singing. I saw a woman gathering flowers. I saw some children dancing. A group of dancing children.

To earn, *guadagnare;* to teach, *insegnare;* to drown, *affogare;* to cross, *attraversare;* to waver, *ondeggiare;* I hear, *odo;* I saw, *vidi;* to gather, *cogliere;* to dance, *danzare* or *ballare;* living, *vitto;* river, *fiume;* mortal, *mortale;* hope, *speranza;* fear, *timore;* woman, *donna;* flower, *fiori;* group, *gruppo;* child, *fanciullo.*

XVII.—IRREGULAR VERBS.

FIRST CONJUGATION.

1. The Imperfect, Indicative, and Subjunctive, the Gerund, and the second person plural of the Present Indicative, are almost always regular in all conjugations.

2. The second person singular, the first and second plural of the preterit are always regular. Ex.: from *piangere*, to weep.

PRET.—piansi, *piangesti*, pianse, *piangemmo, piangeste*, piansero.

3. The future and conditional are always regular, though sometimes subject to contraction. Ex.: from *vedere*, to see. Fut. vedrò; Cond. vedrei.—From *tenere*, to hold. Fut. terrò; Cond. terrei; both tenses are regular throughout all persons, as to termination.

Fut. *vedrò, vedrai, vedrà, vedremo, vedrete, vedranno.*
Cond. *terrei, terresti, terrebbe, terremmo, terreste, terrebbero.*

4. Any contraction in the Infinitive always runs through the future and conditional. Ex.: *porre* (contr. of *ponere*), to put. Fut. *porrò*, etc.; Cond. *porrei*, etc.

IRREGULAR VERBS.

5. Any irregularity of the Present Indicative always occurs again in the Imperative and Present Subjunctive.

6. Some constant anomalies, chiefly resulting from the laws of euphony occur in verbs, otherwise regular.

1st. Verbs in *c-are* and *g-are* take an *h* before all those terminations which begin by an *e* or an *i*.

Ex. *manc-are*, to fail.

Pr. Ind. *manc-o*, manch-i, *manc-a*, manch-iamo, *manc-ate, manc-ano*.
Imperat. *manc-a*, manch-i, manch-iamo, *manc-ate*, manch-ino.
Subj. Pr. manch-i, 3 persons; manch-iamo, manch-iate, manch-ino.
Fut. manch-erò, manch-erai, etc.; Cond. manch-erei, manch-eresti, etc.

So, *preg-are*, to pray. Pr. Ind. *preg-o*, pregh-i, etc.

2nd. Verbs in *ci-are* and *gi-are* drop the *i* before *i* or *e*.

Ex. *cianci-are*, to chat.

Pr. Ind. *cianci-o*, cianc-i. *cianci-a*, cianc-iamo, *cianci-ate, cianci-ano*.
Imperat. *cianci-a*, cianc-i, cianc-iamo, *cianci-ate*, cianc-ino.
Subj. Pr. cianc-i, 3 pers.; cianc-iamo, cianc-iate, cianc-ino.
Fut. cianc-erò, etc. Cond. cianc-erei, etc.

So, *mangi-are*, to eat. Pr. Ind. *mangi-o*, mang-i, etc.

3rd. Verbs in *gli-are*, and *chi-are*, drop the *i* only before *i*.

Ex. *consigli-are*, to advise.

Pr. Ind. *pigli-o*, pigl-i, etc. Fut. *pigli-erò*, etc.

So, *invecchi-are*, to grow old.

Pr. Ind. *invecchi-o*, invecch-i, etc. Fut. *invecchi-erò*, etc.

4th. Other verbs in *iare* drop the *i* before an *i*, unless that vowel constitutes the whole termination, or unless the accent falls upon it.

Ex. *odi-are*, to hate.

Pr. Ind. *odi-o*, odi-i, *odi-a*, od-iamo, etc.
Imper. *odi-a*, odi-i, odi-amo, *odi-ate*, od-ino.
Subj. Pr. *odi-i*, 3 pers.; od-iamo, od-iate, od-ino.

So, *invi-are*, to send.

Pr. Ind. *invi-o*, *invi-i*, *invi-a*, inv-iamo, *invi-áte*, *invi-ano*.

Imper. *invi-a, invi-i*, inv-iámo, *invi-àte, invi-ino.*
Subj. Pr. *invi-i*, 3 pers.; inv-iamo, inv-iate, *invi-ino.*

5*th.* *Giocare*, to play, takes a *u*, wherever the accent falls upon the *o*.

Pr. Ind. giuóco, giuóchi, giuóca, *giochiàmo, giocàte*, giuócano.
Imper. giuóca, giuóchi, *giochiamo, giocàte*, giuóchino.
Subj. Pr. giuóchi, 3 pers.; *giochiamo, giochiate*, giuóchino.

So, likewise, *arrolare*, to enlist; *rotare*, to wheel; *sonare*, to play; *rinnovare*, to renew; *infocare*, to inflame, etc., etc. The same anomalies occur also in the second conjugation. See *cuocere, muovere*, etc.

7. There are only three irregular verbs of the first conjugation.

1*st.* *Andare*, to go. Ger. *andando*, going. P.P. *andato*, gone (neut. pass.)
Pr. Ind. vo, *or* vado, vai, va, *andiamo, andate,* vanno.
Imp. *andava.* Pret. *andai.* Fut. *andrò,* or *anderò,* etc. Cond. andrei, or *anderei*, etc.
Imper. va, vada, *andiamo, andate,* vadano.
Subj. Pr. vada, 3 pers.; *andiamo, andiate,* vadano. Imp. *andassi.*

(*Andare*, like all neuter passive verbs, has its compound tenses conjugated with *essere, sono andato, era andato,* I have gone, I was gone, &c.)

Trasandare, to exceed or neglect, and *riandare*, to go over again or consider, both compound of *andare* are, however, regular.

Pr. Ind. *trasando, trasandi,* &c.

2*nd.* *Dare,* to give. Ger. *dando.* P.P. *dato,* (act. verb.)
Pr. Ind. do, dai, dà, *diamo, date,* danno. Imp. *dava.*
Pret. diedi, *or* detti, desti, diede, *or* dette, demmo, deste, diedero, *or* dettero. Fut. darò, etc. Cond. darei, etc.
Imper. dà, dia, *diamo, date,* diano.
Subj. Pr. dia, 3 pers.; *diamo, diate,* diano. Imp. dessi, dessi, etc.

Ridare, to give again, *addarsi*, to perceive, conjugated like *dare*.

3rd. Stare, to stay or stand, all conjugated like *dare*, (neut. pass.) Ger. *stando*. P. P. *stato*.
Pr. Ind. *sto, stai*, etc. Imp. *stava*. Pret. *stetti, stesti, stette, stemmo, steste, stettero*. Fut. *starò*, etc. Cond. *starei*, etc.
Imper. *sta, stia*, etc.
Pr. Sub. *stia*, etc. Imp. *stessi*, etc.

Ristare, to stop; *distare*, to be distant; *soprastare*, to temporise, are all conjugated like *stare*.

Soprastare, or *sovrastare*, to rule, or to impend, is regular throughout.
Pr. Ind. *sovrasto, sovrasti*, etc.

Exercise.

I think that some one is missing, (subj. pr.) Two pages are missing. We have given our word, and shall not fail. You will soon weary of my company. They would beg him in vain. Thou fearest that I may avenge myself. I must find some one that will bind (subj. pr.) me these books.

To think, *credere*; to be missing, *mancare*; to fail, *mancare*; to weary, *stancare*; to beg, *pregare*; to avenge, *vendicare*; to bind, *legare*; I must find, *bisogna ch' io trovi*; some one, *qualcuno*; page, *pagina*; word, *parola*; company, *compagnia*; book, *libro*; in vain, *indarno*.

Why do you quarrel? I do not know why they quarrel. (sub. pr.) Thus dost thou leave me? I will never leave thee in peace. If thou dost not eat these apples, the pigs will eat them. Tell them to leave me (that they may leave me) in peace. It is necessary that thou shouldst take (subj. pr.) this medicine. Be sure that we do not hate thee. How can I be sure that thou dost not hate me? I shall hate thee if thou hatest me. I care not whether they hate or love me, (subj. pr.)

To quarrel, *litigare*; I do not know why, *non so perché*; to leave, *lasciare*; to eat, *mangiare*; it is necessary, *bisogna;* to hate, *odiare;* be sure that, *sii certo che;* how can I be sure that, *come posso esser certo che?* I care not whether, *non mi importa che;* never, *non-mai;* apple, *mela;* pig, *porco;* peace, *pace;* medicine, *medicina.*

Birds renew their feathers every year. I play hearts and thou playest diamonds. Play and I will sing. Sing and I will play. Give me the horse and walk. I ride and he walks. Where are you going? Where are those pilgrims going? Where were you going when I met you? Where did you go yesterday? He promenades all day and neglects his business. He is gone away. Do (you) not go away. Tell (to) him he may go (subj. pr.) Tell him he may go away. Go into the ante-chamber, but do not go away. He gave me his orders, and then went home. Give him your orders, and he shall go away. The best friends go away and leave me alone.

To renew, *rinnovare;* to play (cards), *giocare;* to play (music), *sonare;* to go, *andare;* to walk, *andare a piedi;* to ride, *andare a cavallo;* to promenade, *andare a spasso;* to go away, *andarsene;* to meet, *incontrare;* to neglect, *trasandare;* tell, *dite;* bird, *uccello;* feather, *penna;* hearts, *cuori;* diamonds, *quadri,* or *denari;* pilgrim, *pellegrino;* where, *dove;* yesterday, *ieri;* when, *quando;* business, *affare* (in plur.); ante-chamber, *anticamera;* order, *ordine;* home, *a casa;* then, *poi;* alone, *solo.*

Where do you live? The doctor lives in the same street. How do you do? I am very well. How is your mother? She was quite well when I left her. He stood in suspense. How long will you stay in this country? Let us look on. Go to my father's, he will give you some letters. These are the letters he gave me.

To live (to dwell), *stare (di casa);* to do, to be, in health, *stare (di salute);* to stand, *stare;* in suspense, *sospeso;* to stay, *stare;* to look on, *stare a vedere.*

To my father's, at my father's, (*da mio padre*); the Italian *da* is used to correspond to the French *chez*.

Doctor, *medico*; street, *strada*; how, *come*; country, *paese*; letter, *lettera*; how long, *quanto*, or *quanto tempo*.

He gives (to) me back what he has stolen from (to) me. If they perceive (of) your intentions, they will go away. I have not perceived (of) the trick. Good Christians give all to the poor. He gave himself much trouble. I have given myself no great trouble.

To give back, *ri-dare*; to steal, *rubare*; to perceive, *ad-darsi*; intention, *intenzione*; trick, *scherzo*; poor, *povero*, in plur.; trouble, *disturbo*.

What threatens me? These are the calamities that hang over us. If they hesitate, they are lost. I do not know where it begins, (subj. pr.) I do not hope that they will change, (subj. pr.) The more he reviews the past, the more he finds it strange. You will fatigue yourself. You will change your mind, if you think it over again.

To threaten, to hang over, to hesitate, *sovra-stare*; to lose, *perdere*; to begin, *cominciare*; to hope, *sperare*; to change, *cangiare*; to review, *ri-andare*; to find, *trovare*; to fatigue, *stancare*; to change one's mind, *cangiar d' idea*; to think over again, *ripensare*; it (to it), *ci*; I do not know, *non so*; the more, *più*; strange, *strano*; the past, *il passato*; calamity, *sciagura*.

XVIII.—IRREGULAR VERBS.
SECOND CONJUGATION.

1. The following are the only regular verbs of the second conjugation.

battere,	to beat.	*pendere*,	to hang.
cedere,	to yield.	*perdere*,	to lose.

compiere,	to accomplish.	*premere,*	to press.
credere,	to believe.	*ricevere,*	to receive.
fendere,	to cleave.	*riflettere,*	to reflect.
fremere,	to fret, or rage.	*ripetere,*	to repeat.
gemere,	to groan.	*splendere,*	to shine.
godére,	to enjoy.	*temére,*	to fear.
mescere,	to mix.	*tondere,*	to shear.
mietere,	to reap.	*vendere,*	to sell.
pascere,	to feed.		

(*a*) The verbs *assistere, esistere, consistere,* are regular, with the exception of the past participle, *assistito, esistito,* &c.

(*b*) *Cedere* has the preterit *cessi* besides *cedei; perdere* has two preterits, *persi* or *perdei,* and two past participles, *perso* or *perduto.*

(*c*) *Appendere,* compound of *pendere,* has pret. *appesi;* past. par. *appeso.*

(*d*) *Riflettere* is regular when it means to reflect, to consider; but it has pret. *riflessi,* and past. par. *riflesso,* when it means to reverberate.

2. Some of the verbs of the second conjugation, such as *cuocere,* to cook ; *muovere,* to move ; have an anomaly in the present, in the imperative, and present subjunctive, analogous to what we have seen in the first conjugation respecting the verb *giocare,* that is, they take a *u* whenever the accent falls upon the *o.*

  Ex. cuócere, to cook ; Ger. *cocèndo* ; P. P. cotto.
Pr. In. cuóco, cuóci, cuóce, *cociámo, cocète,* cuócono.
Imper. cuóci, cuóca, *cociámo, cocète, cuócano.*
Sub. Pr. cuóca, 3 persons ; *cociámo, cociáte,* cuócano.

3. A great number of verbs of the second conjugation have irregular preterits and past participles.

The irregularity of the preterit, is, however, as we have said, confined to the 1st and 3rd person singular, and 3rd plural.

  Ex. from *cuocere,* to cook.
Pret. cossi, *cocesti,* cosse, *cocemmo, coceste,* cossero.

4. The following table contains the most frequent anomalies.

 a **trarre, (traere,)* Pret. *trassi,* P. P. *tratto,* to draw.

IRREGULAR VERBS.

b	assorbere,	assorsi,	assorto,	to absorb.
	*tacére,	tacqui,	taciuto,	to be silent.
	*condurre,	(conducere,) condussi,		condotto, to guide.
	*fare,	(facere,)	feci,	fatto, to do or make.
	*dire,	(dicere,)	dissi,	detto, to tell or say.
	rilucere,	rilussi,		to shine.
c	*cuocere,	cossi,	cotto,	to cook.
	vincere,	vinsi,	vinto,	to conquer.
	torcere,	torsi,	torto,	to twist.
	nuocere,	nocqui,	nociuto,	to hurt or injure.
	nascere,	nacqui,	nato,	to be born.
	crescere,	crebbi,	cresciuto,	to grow.
	conoscere,	conobbi,	conosciuto, to know.	
	*cadere,	caddi,	caduto,	to fall.
	*vedere,	vidi,	veduto,	to see.
	persuadere, persuasi,		persuaso,	to persuade.
	invadere,	invasi,	invaso,	to invade.
	cedere,	cessi, or	cedei,	ceduto, to yield.
	ledere,	lesi,	leso,	to hurt, to violate.
	chiedere,	chiesi,	chiesto,	to ask.
	ridere,	risi,	riso,	to laugh.
	rodere,	rosi,	roso,	to gnaw.
d	chiudere,	chiusi,	chiuso,	to shut.
	ardere,	arsi,	arso,	to burn.
	perdere,	perdei, or	persi,	perso, or perduto, to lose.
	sperdere,	spersi,	sperso,	to disperse.
	mordere,	morsi,	morso,	to bite.
	spendere,	spesi,	speso,	to spend.
	scindere,	scinsi,	scinto,	to sever.
	nascondere, nascosi,		nascoso, or nascosto, to hide.	
	fondere,	fusi,	fuso,	to melt.
	esigere,	esigei,	esatto,	to exact.
g	dirigere,	diressi,	diretto,	to direct.
	leggere,	lessi,	letto,	to read.
	affiggere,	affissi,	affitto,	to affix, to stick up.

88 ITALIAN GRAMMAR.

	affliggere,	afflissi,	afflitto,	to afflict.
	distruggere,	distrussi,	distrutto,	to destroy.
	piangere,	piansi,	pianto,	to weep.
	*spegnere,	(spengere,)	spensi,	spento, to quench.
	cingere,	cinsi,	cinto,	to gird.
g	stringere,	strinsi,	stretto,	to press.
	ungere,	unsi,	unto,	to anoint.
	spargere,	sparsi,	sparso,	to spread.
	ergere,	ersi,	erto, or	eretto, to erect.
	aspergere,	aspersi,	asperso,	to sprinkle.
	sorgere,	sorsi,	sorto,	to rise.
gu	estinguere,	estinsi,	estinto,	to extinguish.
	*valére,	valsi,	valso, or	valuto, to be worth.
	*dolére,	dolsi,	doluto,	to pain or grieve.
l	*volére,	volli,	voluto,	to wish.
	svellere,	svelsi,	svelto,	to uproot.
	espellere,	espulsi,	espulso,	to expel.
gli	*scegliere,	scelsi,	scelto,	to choose.
	*cogliere,	colsi,	colto,	to gather.
	esprimere,	espressi,	espresso,	to express.
m	redimere,	redensi, or	redimei,	redento, to redeem.
	assumere,	assunsi,	assunto,	to assume.
	*rimanére,	rimasi,	rimaso, or	rimasto, to remain.
	*tenére,	tenni,	tenuto,	to hold or keep.
n	*porre,	(ponere,)	posi,	posto, to put.
	scernere,	scersi, or	scernei,	scerso, or scernuto, to discern.
p	*sapére,	seppi,	saputo,	to know.
	rompere,	ruppi,	rotto,	to break.
r	*parére,	parvi, or	parsi,	parso, or paruto, to appear.
	correre,	corsi,	corso,	to run.
	scuotere,	scossi,	scosso,	to shake.
t	discutere,	discussi,	discusso,	to disuse.
	connettere,	connessi,	connesso,	to connect.
	mettere,	misi,	messo,	to put.

IRREGULAR VERBS. 89

	*bere,	(bevere,)	bevvi, or bevei,	bevuto, to drink.
	vivere,	vissi,	vissuto, or	vivuto, to live.
v	scrivere,	scrissi,	scritto,	to write.
	muovere,	mossi,	mosso,	to move.
	piovere,	piovvi,	piovuto,	to rain.
	assolvere,	assolsi,	assolto,	to absolve.
	risolvere,	risolsi,	risoluto,	to resolve.

* All verbs marked thus have other irregularities besides the preterit and past participle. (See the following lessons.)

Exercise.

The door is shut. The meat is cooked. Here she was born and grew up. Here she saw and conquered. I knew him when he was in France. How much have you spent? What profit have you drawn from it? He shone by reflected light.

To shut, *chiudere;* to cook, *cuocere;* to be born, *nascere;* to grow up, *crescere;* to see, *vedere;* to conquer, *vincere;* to know, *conoscere;* to spend, *spendere;* to draw, *trarre;* to shine, *splendere;* to reflect, *riflettere;* door, *porta;* meat, *carne;* how much, *quanto;* what profit, *che guadagno;* light, *luce.*

It rained all day. She moved me to tears. He has described the scene as it happened. She survived (to) her husband. They have succoured him. He ran over many countries. He laid very hard terms upon the conquered. Are you convinced? You will be expelled.

To rain, *piovere;* to move, *muovere;* to describe, *descrivere;* to happen, *ac-cadere;* to survive, *sopravvivere;* to succour, *soc-correre;* to run over, *per-correre;* to lay, *im-porre;* to convince, *con-vincere;* to expel, *espellere;* to tears, *al pianto;* scene, *scena;* husband, *marito;* country, *paese;* term, *patto;* hard, *duro;* upon, *to.*

In the year that Troy was burnt. He laughed when I asked (to) him where he had hid himself. She held the

I 3

child grasped in her arms. The people shook off the yoke. She lived very happy with him. We all wept when we saw her smile. She smiled when she saw us weep. We were all confused and overcome. He betted for the black horse. We pitied him. He pitied us. They are gnawed by envy. Are you disposed to forgive (to) him? He was surrounded by the enemies who slew him without resistance.

To burn, *ardere*; to laugh, *ridere*; to ask, *chiedere*; to hide, *nascondere*; to hold, *tenere*; to grasp, *stringere*; to shake off, *scuotere*; to live, *vivere*; to weep, *piangere*; to smile, *sor-ridere*; to confuse, *con-fondere*; to overcome, *sopraf-fare*; to bet, *scom-mettere*; to pity, *com-piangere*; to gnaw, *rodere*; to dispose, *di-sporre*; to forgive, *perdonare*; to surround, *cingere*; to slay, *uccidere*; Troy, *Troia*; arm, *braccio*; yoke, *giogo*; envy, *invidia*; people, *popolo* (sing); resistance, *difesa*; without, *senza*; happy, *felice*.

XIX.—IRREGULAR VERBS.

SECOND CONJUGATION.

1. Besides the anomalies in the preterit and past participle, some verbs of the second conjugation have the following irregularities.

2. Verbs with an *a* preceding the termination *ere*.

Trarre, to draw, (contr. of *traere*,) act. ver. Ger. *traendo*.
P. P. tratto.
Pr. Ind. traggo, trai or traggi, trae or tragge, traggiamo, traete, traggono.
Imp. traeva. Pret. trassi, traesti, &c. Fut. trarrò, &c. Cond. trarrei, &c.

Imper. *trai*, tragga, traggiamo, *traete*, traggano.
Sub. Pr. tragga, 3 pers.; traggiamo, traggiate, traggano.
Imp. *traessi*.
Conjugate alike—*estrarre*, to extract; *contrarre*, to contract; *sottrarre*, to withdraw, &c.

3. Verbs with a *c* before *ere*.
Condurre, contr. of *conducere*, to lead. Ger. *conducendo*.
P. P. *condotto*, active verb.
Pr. Ind. *conduco*. Imp. *conduceva*. Pret. condussi, *conducesti*, &c. Fut. condurrò, &c. Cond. condurrei, &c. Imp. *conduci*. Subj. Pr. *conduca*. Imp. *conducessi*.

(No irregularity, save in the preterit and participle past, and contraction in the infinitive, future, and conditional.)

So—*indurre*, to induce; *tradurre*, to translate; *sedurre*, to seduce; *introdurre*, to introduce, &c. &c.; *ridurre*, to reduce.

Dire, (contr. of *dicere*,) to say (active verb). Ger. *dicendo*.
P. P. detto.
Pr. Ind. dico, dici, or dì, *dice*, *diciamo*, dite, *dicono*. Imp. *diceva*.
Pret. dissi, *dicesti*, &c. Fut. dirò, &c. Cond. direi, &c.
Imper. dì, *dica*, *diciamo*, dite, *dicano*.
Subj. Pr. *dica*, 3 pers.; *diciamo*, *diciate*, *dicano*. Imp. *dicessi*.

So—*ridire*, to repeat; *disdire*, to unsay; *predire*, to foretell; *contraddire*, to contradict; *benedire*, to bless; *maledire*, to curse, &c.

Fare, (contr. of *facere*,) to do, or make. Ger. *facendo*.
P. P. fatto.
Pr. Ind. fo, *or* faccio, fai, fa, facciamo, fate, fanno. Imp. *faceva*.
Pret. feci, *facesti*, &c. Fut. farò, &c. Cond. farei, &c.
Imper. fa, faccia, facciamo, fate, facciano.
Subj. Pr. faccia, 3 pers.; facciamo, facciate, facciano. Imp. *facessi*.

So—*rifare*, to do again; *disfare*, to undo; *confare*, to suit; *assuefare*, to accustom; *contraffare*, to counterfeit; *soddisfare*, to satisfy, &c.

Piacere, to please (neut. v.) Ger. *piacendo*. P. P. piaciuto.

Pr. Ind. piaccio, *piaci, piace*, piacciamo, *piacete*, piacciono.
Imp. *piaceva*.
Pret. piacqui, *piacesti*, &c. Fut. *piacerò*. Cond. *piacerei*.
Imper. *piaci*, piaccia, piacciamo, *piacete*, piacciano.
Subj. Pr. piaccia, 3 pers.; piacciamo, piacciate, piacciano.
Imp. *piacessi*.

So—*compiacere*, to please; *dispiacere*, to displease.
giacere, to lie down; *soggiacere*, to succumb.
tacere, to be silent; (some of the irregular persons of this verb may be written with one *c*, as *taciamo*, we are silent.)

4. Verbs with a *d* before *ere*.

Cadere, to fall, (neut. pass.) Ger. *cadendo*. P. P. *caduto*.
Pr. Ind. *cado*, or caggio, *cadi, cade, cadiamo*, or caggiamo, *cadete, cadono*, or caggiono. Imp. *cadeva*.
Pret. caddi, *cadesti*, &c. Fut. cadrò, &c. Cond. cadrei, &c.
Imper. *cadi, cada*, or *caggia, cadiamo*, or caggiamo, *cadete, cadano*, or *caggiano*.
Subj. Pr. *cada*, or caggia, 3 pers.; *cadiamo*, or caggiamo, *cadiate*, or caggiate, *cadano*, or caggiano. Imp. *cadessi*.

So—*scadere*, to fall of; *accadere*, to happen; *ricadere*, to fall again, &c.

Vedere, to see (active verb.) Ger. *vedendo*. P. P. *veduto*.
Ind. Pr. *vedo*, veggo, *or* veggio, *vedi, vede, vediamo*, or veggiamo, *vedete, vedono*, or veggono, or veggiono. Imp. *vedeva*. Fut. vedrò, &c. Cond. vedrei, &c.
Imper. *vedi, veda*, or vegga, or veggia, *vediamo*, or veggiamo, *vedete, vedano*, or veggano, or veggiano.

Subj. Pr. *veda*, *vegga*, *or* *veggia*, 3 pers.; *vediamo*, or *veggiamo*, *vediate*, or *veggiate*, *vedano*, *veggano*, or *veggiano*. Imp. *vedessi*.

So—*rivedere*, to see again; *avvedere*, to perceive; *divedere*, *travedere*, &c.; *provvedere*, to provide; and *prevedere*, to foresee; are not contracted in the future and cond.; *provvederò*, *prevederei*, not *provvedrò*, &c.

Sedere, to sit (neut. verb.) Ger. *sedendo*. P. P. *seduto*.

Pr. Ind. siedo, seggo, *or* seggio, siedi, siede, *sediamo*, or seggiamo, *sedete*, siedono, or seggono, or seggiono. Imp. *sedeva*. Pret. *sedei*. Fut. *sederò*. Cond. *sederei*.

Imper. siedi, sieda, *or* segga, *sediamo*, or seggiamo, *sedete*, siedano, *or* seggano.

Subj. Pr sieda, segga, *or* seggia, 3 pers.; *sediamo*, or seggiamo, *sediate*, or seggiate, siedano, seggano, seggiano. Imp. *sedessi*.

So—*risedere*, to reside; *presedere*, to preside; *possedere*, to possess; *soprassedere*, to temporise.

Exercise.

They drag him to death. Whilst they were dragging him to death, his friends came up and withdrew him from their fury. From this field I draw all my sustenance. He drew his sword and ran him through.

To drag, *trarre*; to come up, *sopraggiungere*; to withdraw, *sottrarre*; withdraw from (withdraw to); to draw, *trarre*; to run through, *trafiggere*; death, *morte*; whilst, *mentre*; fury, *furore*; field, *campo*; sustenance, *sostentamento*; sword, *spada*.

See what you have brought him to. His friends led him astray. They will guide you on the right way. The father's rigour produced its wonted effect. What sayest thou? Why doest thou not do what thou sayest? What he said he did. You have undone all the good you had done.

To see, *vedere*; to bring, *indurre*; to lead astray, *sedurre*; to guide, *condurre*; to produce, *produrre*; to say, *dire;* to do, *fare;* to undo, *disfare;* the right way, *il buon sentiero;* wonted effect, *usato effetto.*

Do it again and perhaps you will do it better. They do everything in too great a hurry. They satisfy nobody. You will be satisfied. You were accustoming yourself to our climate. Do not contradict me. All the poor bless him. His work was blessed. Blessed be his holy name.

To do again, *rifare;* to satisfy, *soddisfare;* to accustom, *assuefare;* to contradict, *contraddire;* to bless, *benedire;* perhaps, *forse;* in too great a hurry, *con troppa fretta;* climate, *clima;* work, *lavoro;* holy name, *santo nome.*

Do what you please (pleases you). I like her (she pleases to me) but she does not like me. I like all your sisters. In what do I displease you? From the first moment that she pleased (to) me. For some time I was pleased with (of) his company. There lie our forefathers.

To like, *piacere;* (invert every sentence,) to displease, *dispiacere;* to be pleased, *compiacersi;* to lie, *giacere;* sister, *sorella;* forefathers, *maggiori;* moment, *istante;* time, *tempo.*

He was silent for the rest of the day. Our warriors lay scattered about the battle-field. They sank overwhelmed by the heat of the day. They succumbed under (to) so many attacks. That very pure soul was silent. They will oblige you. Let them both be silent.

To be silent, *tacere;* to lie, *giacere;* to scatter, *spargere;* to sink, *cadere;* to overwhelm, *opprimere;* to succumb, *soggiacere;* to oblige, *compiacere;* the rest, *il rimanente;* warrior, *guerriero;* about, *per;* battle field, *campo;* heat, *calore;* day, *giornata;* attack, *assalto;* pure, *onesto;* soul, *anima;* both, *entrambi.*

There were the ruins lying. Some were sitting, some lying down. Tell them that they may sit down (subj. pr.) He did not permit that he should sit down (subj. imp.)

To permit, *permettere;* to sit down, *sedere;* ruin, *rovina;* Do as (what) I say, not as (what) I do. Do you see what

IRREGULAR VERBS.

I am doing? I see what you are doing. They are doing their duty. Some sit, some lie on the ground. If you sit on that stool you will fall. These things happen sometimes. What has happened to you?

To see, *vedere;* I am doing, (I do, or I *stay doing;*) to fall, *cadere;* to happen, *accadere* (neut. pass.); duty, *dovere;* ground, *suolo;* stool, *scanno;* sometime, *talvolta.*

It happened one day that the children were making a great noise. He bowed down his head and was silent He was sitting on the ground and held his peace. The town sits on the sea shore. She who sitteth upon the waters. They sit on his left (hand).

To make, *fare;* to bow, *chinare;* to hold his peace, *tacere;* child, *fanciullo;* noise, *romore;* head, *fronte;* ground, *suolo;* town, *città;* sea-shore, *marina;* left, *sinistro;* on his left, (at his left,) fem.

What will your father say? Shall I ever see her? They will provide all that is needful. They foresaw what soon afterwards happened. What will your friends do? I foresee great misfortunes. I never saw him again. We shall see.

To provide, *provvedere;* to be needful, *abbisognare;* to foresee, *prevedere;* to see again, *rivedere;* soon afterwards, *poco dopo;* misfortune, *sciagura;* never again, (*non mai,*) I never saw him again, (I not him saw again.)

Sit (thou) down and speak. I beg you to sit down. This is the road that leads to honours. This road will take me to town. What have I done? What didst thou say? What shall I do? They say the peace is made. Do you like flowers? Which of these flowers do you like best? I know whom you like.

To speak, *favellare;* to beg, *pregare;* to sit down, (that you may sit down,) (subj. pr.); to lead, to take, *condurre;* to like, *piacere.* Do you like flowers? (do flowers please to you?) (to you please the flowers?) I know, *so;* road, *via,* or *strada;* peace, *pace;* flower, *fiore;* best, *più.*

XX.—IRREGULAR VERBS.

SECOND CONJUGATION.

1. Verbs with a *g* before *ere.*

Spegnere (spengere) to quench (act.) Ger. *spegnendo.* P. P. spento.
Pr. Ind. spengo, *spegni, spegne, spegniamo, spegnete,* spengono.
Imp. *spegneva.* Pret. spensi, *spegnesti,* &c. Fut. *spegnerò.* Cond. *spegnerei.*
Imper. *spegni,* spenga, *spegniamo, spegnete,* spengano.
Subj. Pr. spenga, 3 pers.; *spegniamo, spegniate,* spengano. Imp. *spegnessi.*

Cingere, to gird; *tingere,* to die, &c. &c. are regular, all but the Pret. and P. P.; but some of their persons, besides the regular termination *cinge, tinge,* have also cigne, tigne.

2. Verbs with *l* before *ere.*

Valére, to be worth (neut.) Ger. valendo. P. P. *valuto.* or valso.
Pr. Ind. valgo, *or* vaglio, *vali, vale,* vagliamo, *valete,* valgono, *or* vagliono.
Imp. *valeva.* Pret. valsi, *valesti,* &c. Fut. varrò, &c. Cond. varrei, &c.
Imper. *vali,* valga, *or* vaglia, vagliamo, *valete,* valgano, *or* vagliano.
Subj. Pr. valga, *or* vaglia, 3 pers.; vagliamo, vagliate, valgano, *or* vagliano. Imp. *valessi.*

So—*prevalere,* to prevail; *equivalere,* to be equivalent, &c.

IRREGULAR VERBS.

Dolére, to grieve (reflect.) Ger. *dolendo*. P. P. *doluto*.
Pr. Ind. dolgo, *or* doglio, duoli, duole, dogliamo, *dolete*, dolgono, *or* dogliono.
Imp. *doleva*. Pret. dolsi, *dolesti*, &c. Fut. dorrò, &c. Cond. dorrei, &c.
Imper. duoli, dolga, *or* doglia, dogliamo, *dolete*, dolgano, *or* dogliano.
Subj. Pr. dolga, *or* doglia, 3 pers.; dogliamo, dogliate, dolgano, *or* dogliano. Imp. *dolessi*.
So—*condolere*, to condole, &c.

Volere, to be willing. Ger. *volendo*. P. P. *voluto*.
Pr. Ind. voglio, vuoi, vuole, vogliamo, *volete*, vogliono.
Imp. *voleva*.
Pret. volli, *volesti*, &c. Fut. vorrò. Cond. vorrei. (No imperative.)
Subj. Pr. voglia, 3 pers.; vogliamo, vogliate, vogliano.
Imp. *volessi*.
So—*disvolere*, to change one's mind.

Solére, to be wont. Ger. *solendo*. P. P. solito (a defective verb).
Pr. Ind. soglio, suoli, suole, sogliamo, *solete*, sogliono.
Imp. *soleva*.
Subj. Pr. soglia, 3 pers.; sogliamo, sogliate, sogliano.
Imp. *solessi*. (No other tenses.)

Svellere, to tear up. Ger. *svellendo*. P. P. svelto (act.)
Pr. Ind. svelgo, or *svello, svelli, svelle, svelliamo, svellete*, svelgono.
Imp. *svelleva*. Pret. svelsi, *svellesti*, &c. Fut. *svellerò*. Cond. *svellerei*.
Imper. *svelli*, svelga, *svelliamo, svellete*, svelgano.
Subj. Pr. svelga, or *svella, svelliamo, svelliate*, svelgano.
Imp. *svellessi*.
So—*divellere*.

3. Verbs with *gli* before *ere*.

Scegliere, or scerre, to choose (act.) Ger. *scegliendo*. P. P. scelto.

K

Pr. Ind. scelgo, *scegli, sceglie, scegliamo, scegliete,* scelgono.
Imp. *sceglieva.*
Pret. scelsi, *scegliesti,* &c. Fut. *sceglierò.* Cond. *sceglierei.*
Imper. *scegli,* scelga, *scegliamo, scegliete,* scelgano.
Subj. Pr. scelga, 3 pers.; *scegliamo, scegliate,* scelgano.
Subj. *scegliessi.*
Togliere, or torre, to take (act.) Ger. *togliendo.* P. P. tolto.
Pr. Ind. tolgo, or *toglio, togli, toglie, togliamo, togliete,*
tolgono, or *togliono.*
Imp. *toglieva.* Pret. tolsi, *togliesti,* &c. Fut. *toglierò,*
or torrò. Cond. *toglierei,* or torrei, &c. Imp. *togli,*
tolga, or *toglia,* &c.
Subj. Pr. tolga, or *toglia,* 3 pers.; *togliamo, togliate,* tolgano,
or *togliano.* Imp *togliessi.*
(So—*cogliere,* to gather; *sciogliere,* to loosen, &c. &c.)
4. Verbs with *n* before *ere.*
Rimanére, to remain (neut. pass.) Ger. *rimanendo.* P. P.
rimaso, *or* rimasto.
Pr. Ind. rimango, *rimani, rimane, rimaniamo, rimanete,*
rimangono.
Imp. *rimaneva.* Pret. rimasi, *rimanesti,* &c. Fut. rimarrò, &c. Cond. rimarrei, &c.
Imper. *rimani,* rimanga, *rimaniamo, rimanete,* rimangano.
Subj. Pr. rimanga, 3 pers.; *rimaniamo, rimaniate,* rimangano.
Imp. *rimanessi.*
Porre, cont. of *ponere,* to put (act.) Ger. *ponendo.*
P. P. posto.
Pr. Ind. pongo, *poni, pone, poniamo, ponete,* pongono.
Imp. *poneva.*
Pret. posi, *ponesti,* &c. Fut. porrò, &c. Cond. porrei, &c.
Imper. *poni,* ponga, *poniamo, ponete,* pongano.
Subj. Pr. ponga, 3 pers.; *poniamo, poniate,* pongano.
Imp. *ponessi.*
(So—*opporre, proporre, disporre, supporre, comporre,* &c.)
Tenere, to hold (act.) Ger. *tenendo.* P. P. tenuto.
Pr. Ind. tengo, tieni, tiene, *teniamo, tenete,* tengono.

IRREGULAR VERBS.

Imp.   *teneva.*
Pret.   tenni, *tenesti*, &c. Fut. terrò, &c. Cond. terrei, &c.
Imper.   tieni, tenga, *teniamo, tenete,* tengano.
Subj. Pr. tenga, 3 pers. ; *teniamo, teniate,* tengano.
Imp.   *tenessi.*
(So—*ottenere, mantenere, contenere, sostenere,* &c.)

5. Verbs with *p* before *ere.*

Sapére, to know. Ger. *sapendo.* P. P. *saputo* (neut. act.) (analogous to *avere.*)

Pr. Ind. so, sai, sa, sappiamo, *sapete,* sanno   Imp. *sapeva.*
Pret.   seppi, *sapesti,* &c. Fut. saprò, &c. Cond. saprei, &c.
Imper.   sappi, sappia, sappiamo, sappiate, sappiano.
Subj. Pr. sappia, 3 pers.; sappiamo, sappiate, sappiano.
Imp.   *sapessi.*

6. Verbs with *r* before *ere.*

Parére, to seem (neut.) Ger. *parendo.* P. P. *paruto, or* parso.

Pr. Ind. paio, *pari, pare, pariamo, or* paiamo, *parete,* paiono. Imp. *pareva.*
Pret.   parvi, *paresti,* &c. Fut. parrò, &c. Cond. parrei, &c.
Imper, *pari,* paia, *pariamo, or* paiamo, *parete,* paiano.
Subj. Pr. paia, 3 pers.; *pariamo, or* paiamo, paiate, paiano.
Imp. *paressi.*

7. Verbs with *t* before *ere.*

Potére, to be able (neut. act.) Ger. *potendo.* P. P. *potuto.*

Pr. Ind. posso, puoi, può, possiamo, *potete,* possono.
Imp.   *poteva.*
Pret.   *potei.* Fut. potrò, &c. Cond. potrei, &c. (No Imperative.)
Subj. Pr. possa, 3 pers.; possiamo, possiate, possano.
Imp.   *potessi.*

8. Verbs with *v* before *ere.*

Dovére, to owe. Ger. *dovendo.* P. P. *dovuto.* (neut. act.)

Pr. Ind. devo, debbo, *or* deggio, devi, *or* dei, deve, *or* dee, dobbiamo, *or* deggiamo, *dovete*, debbono, *or* deggiono, *or* devono, *or* deono, *or* denno.
Imp. *doveva.* Pret. *dovetti.* Fut. dovrò. Cond. dovrei, &c. (No Imperative.)
Subj. Pr. deva, debba, *or* deggia, 3 pers.; dobbiamo, *or* deggiamo, dobbiate, *or* deggiate, debbano, or deggiano.
Imp. *dovessi.*

Bere, or *bevere*, to drink (act.) Ger. *bevendo.* P. P. *bevuto.*
Pr. Ind. bevo, *or* beo, bevi, *or* bei, beve, *or* bee, *beviamo, bevete,* &c.
Imp. *beveva.* Pret. *bevei, bevetti,* or bevvi, *bevesti,* &c. Fut. berò. Cond. berei, &c.
(The *v* may be suppressed in most persons.)

Exercise.

Do what thou canst. He who does what he can does what he ought, (pres. ind.) He owes me all he knows. They owe me all they know. I put all my hope in thee. They always choose the best. I remained in that country for a month. I quench my thirst in the pure water.

Can, *potere;* ought, *dovere;* owe, *dovere;* to know, *sapere;* to put, *porre;* to choose, *scegliere;* to remain, *rimanere;* to quench, *spegnere;* hope, *speranza;* pure water, *acqua chiara;* thirst, *sete.*

What dost thou complain of? I would if I could. Thou couldst if thou wouldst. She says yea and nay a hundred times a day. These horses are not worth a hundred crowns. Man proposes, and God disposes. They suppose it but they do not know it.

To complain, *dolersi;* to will, *volere;* can, *potere;* to say (yea), *volere;* to say (nay), *disvolere;* to be worth, *valere;* to propose, *proporre;* to dispose, *disporre;* to suppose, *supporre;* to know, *sapere;* hundred times a day, *cento volte il giorno;* crown, *scudo.*

I do not think they are (subj. pr.) worth so much. They always choose the worst. If they catch you, they kill you. What have they not taken from (to) me? He sustained his losses with great firmness. They maintain him at their own expense.

To think, *credere* ; to choose, *scegliere* ; to catch, *cogliere* ; to kill, *ammazzare;* to take, *togliere* ; to sustain, *sostenere* ; to maintain, *mantenere* ; loss, *perdita* ; firmness, *fermezza* ; expense, *spesa;* at their own expense, *a proprie spese.*

She never seemed to me so beautiful. They must not repent. As soon as I knew it, I complained of it. My head aches. He has a tooth-ache. The tongue strikes where the tooth aches. More cross than he is wont. They are wont to travel in summer.

To seem, *parere;* must, *dovere;* repent, *pentirsi* ; to know, *sapere;* to complain, *dolersi;* to ache, *dolere;* my head aches (to me aches the head); he has a tooth ache (to him ache the teeth) ; to strike, *battere;* to be wont, *solere;* to travel, *viaggiare;* head, *capo;* tooth, *dente;* tongue, *lingua;* summer, *estate;* cross, *burbero;* more than, *più che non.*

Know (thou) that I never drink water. She is worth more than (of) all the gold in (of) the world, if she loves me. Every one (all) knew that they loved each other. What dost thou want? What do you want? What do those rogues want? Remember (thou of) me and love me. Fare (thee) well.

To know, *sapere* ; to drink, *bere;* to love, *voler bene;* to love each other, *volersi bene;* to want, *volere;* to remember, *ricordarsi di;* to fare well, *star bene;* rogue, *birbante;* water, *acqua.*

I cannot dance. I cannot walk. Walk if you can. Play if you can. Recognise me if thou canst. I'll do all I know and can. We cannot, or one cannot, always do what we wish, or one wishes. We never, or one never, knows what we can do till we try. Do (you) not be willing to deny it to me?

To have power, *potere;* to have the skill, *sapere;* to dance, *ballare;* to walk, *camminare;* to play, *sonare;* to recognise, *riconoscere* or *ravvisare;* to try, *provare;* to be willing, *volere;* to deny, *negare;* till, *finché non.*

XXI.—IRREGULAR VERBS.

THIRD CONJUGATION.

1. The following are the only regular verbs of the third conjugation:—

avvertire,	to warn.	*pentire,*	to repent.
bollire,	to boil.	*sentire,*	to feel.
dormire,	to sleep.	*servire,*	to serve.
fuggire,	to fly.	*sortire,*	to sally out.
partire,	to depart.	*vestire,*	to clothe;

(with their compounds.)

2. Many verbs of this conjugation have the present in *isco.*

Ex. *unire,* to unite.

Pr. Ind. unisco, unisci, unisce, *uniamo, unite,* uniscono.
Imper. unisci, unisca, *uniamo, unite,* uniscano.
Subj. Pr. unisca, 3 pers.; *uniamo, uniate,* uniscano.

3. The following verbs have both the regular termination, and that in *isco.*

abborrire,	to abhor.	*muggire,*	to bellow.
inghiottire,	to swallow.	*ruggire,*	to roar.
languire,	to languish.	*sorbire,*	to sip;
mentire,	to lie.		

(with their compounds.)

4. *Seguire,* to follow, may take an *i* wherever the accent falls upon the *e.*

IRREGULAR VERBS.

Pr. Ind. sieguo, siegui, siegue, *seguiamo, seguite,* sieguono.
Imper. siegui, siegua, &c. Subj. Pr. siegua, &c.
(So—*proseguire,* to continue; *inseguire,* to pursue, &c.)
5. *Salire,* to ascend. Ger. *salendo.* P. P. *salito* (neut.)
Pr. Ind. salgo, *sali, sale,* sagliamo, *salite,* salgono.
Imp. *saliva.*
Pret. *salii,* or salsi, *salisti,* &c. Fut. *salirò.*
Cond. *salirei.*
Imper. *sali,* salga, &c.
Subj. Pr. salga, 3 pers., &c. analogous to *valere.*
(So—*assalire,* to assail; *risalire,* to reascend, &c.)
6. *Apparire* has, besides the termination in *isco,* some persons analogous to *parere.* Ger. apparendo. P. P. apparso.
Pr. Ind. appaio, *appari, appare, appariamo, apparite,* appaiono.
Imp. *appariva.* Pret. apparvi, *apparii,* or apparsi, *apparisti,* &c.
Fut. *apparirò.* Cond. *apparirei.*
Imper. *appari,* appaia, &c. Subj. Pr. appaia, &c.
Imp. *apparissi.*
(So—*sparire,* to disappear, &c.)
7. *Morire,* to die. Ger. *morendo.* P. P. morto (neut. pass.)
Pr. Ind. muoio, *or* muoro, or *moro,* muori, muore, *moriamo, morite,* muoiono, *or* muorono.
Imp. *moriva.* Pret. *morii.* Fut. morrò, or *morirò.*
Cond. morrei, or *morirei.*
Imper. muori, or *mori,* muoia, *or* muora, *moriamo,* &c.
Subj. Pr. *muoia,* or *muora,* 3 pers., &c. Imp. *morissi.*
8. *Venire,* to come. Ger. *venendo.* P. P. *venuto* (neut. pass., analogous to *tenere.*)
Pr. Ind. vengo, vieni, viene, *veniamo, venite,* vengono.
Imp. *veniva.* Pret. venni, *venisti,* &c. Fut. verrò.
Cond. verrei.
Imper. vieni, venga, *veniamo, venite,* vengano.

Subj. Pr. venga, 3 pers.; *veniamo, veniate,* vengano.
Imp. *venissi.*
(So—*svenire,* to faint; *convenire,* to agree, &c.)

9. *Udire,* to hear. Ger. *udendo.* P. P. *udito* (act.)
Pr. Ind. odo, odi, ode, *udiamo, udite,* odono. Fut. udrò, or *udirò.* Cond. udrei, or *udirei.*
Imp. odi, oda, *udiamo, udite,* odano.
Subj. Pr. oda, 3 pers.; *udiamo, udiate,* odano, (regular in all other tenses.)

10. *Uscire,* to go out. Ger. *uscendo.* P. P. *uscito* (neut. pass.)
Pr. Ind. esco, esci, esce, *usciamo, uscite,* escono.
Imper. esci, esca, *usciamo, uscite,* escano.
Subj. Pr. esca, 3 pers.; *usciamo, usciate,* escano, (regular in all other tenses.)
(So—*riuscire,* to succeed.)

11. *Cucire,* to sew, takes an *i* in all terminations in *o* and *a.*
Pr. Ind. cuci-o, *cuc-i, cuc-e, cuc-iamo, cuc-ite, cuci-ono.*
Imper. *cuc-i,* cuci-a, &c.
Subj. Pr. cuci-a, &c.; (otherwise regular.)
(So—*scucire, sdrucire,* to unsew, to rip.)

12. *Empire,* to fill. Ger. *empiendo.* P. P. *empito.*
Pr. Ind. empio, *empi,* empie, *empiamo, empite,* empiono.
Imper. *empi,* empia, &c. Subj. Pr. empia, 3 pers., &c.
Otherwise regular. The irregular persons are from *empiere.*
(So—*compire, adempire,* to fulfil, &c.)

13. *Aprire,* to open.
Pret. *aprii, or* apersi, *apristi,* &c. P. P. **aperto;** (otherwise regular.)
(So—*coprire,* to cover; *offrire,* to offer; *soffrire,* to suffer, &c.)

14. *Istruire,* to instruct. Pret. istrussi, or *istruii;* (otherwise regular.)

15. *Seppellire.* All regular but P. P. sepolto, or *seppellito.*

IRREGULAR VERBS. 105

Exercise.

She fainted when she saw him. She faints every time she sees him. Let them come to-morrow. He goes and comes every week. They go out together every morning. This kind of life does not suit me. They agreed on (at) these conditions.

To faint, *svenire;* to see, *vedere;* to come, *venire;* to go, *andare;* to go out, *uscire;* to suit, *convenire;* to agree, *convenire;* every time, *ogni volta;* to-morrow, *domani;* together, *insieme;* morning, *mattina;* week, *settimana;* kind, *modo;* condition, *patto.*

A thousand fierce doubts assail me. He was twenty years old when he ascended (on) the throne. They sew morning and evening. Out of the water they die. He dies like a Christian. Do not go on; I understand you. Finish thy letter and send it to the post.

To assail, *assalire;* to ascend, *salire;* to sew, *cucire;* to die, *morire;* to go on, *proseguire;* to understand, *capire;* to finish, *finire;* to send, *mandare;* doubt, *dubbio;* fierce, *fiero;* he was twenty years old (he had twenty years); water, *acqua;* out, *fuori;* like a Christian, *da Cristiano;* letter, *lettera;* post, *posta.*

The ghost of his grandmother appeared to him. Ghosts appear at midnight. Leave (thou) me, fearful ghost. Depart, vanish! Here was born, here he died, and was buried. They are long since dead and buried. Do not forsake me when I die, (subj. pr.)

To appear, *apparire;* to leave, *lasciare;* to depart, *uscire;* to vanish, *sparire;* to be born, *nascere;* to die, *morire;* to bury, *seppellire;* to forsake, *abbandonare;* ghost, *ombra;* grandmother, *nonna;* midnight, *mezzanotte;* fearful, *orribile;* here, *qui;* long since, *da gran tempo.*

The door is open. This is the house they have offered to me. This happened before gunpowder was (subj. imp.) discovered. Columbus discovered America towards the end of the fifteenth century. The angels hid their face with their wings. Open the door.

To open, *aprire;* to offer, *offrire;* to happen, *avvenire;* to discover, *scoprire;* to hide, *coprire;* door, *porta,* or *uscio;* house, *casa;* before, *prima che;* gunpowder, *polvere;* Columbus, *Colombo;* end, *fine;* century, *secolo;* towards, *verso;* angel, *angelo;* face, *volto;* wing, *ala;* hid their face (to themselves hid the face).

I must go out. You must hear me. They must hear me. Hear (thou) me. The whole world shall hear it. Those birds come out only by night. After sunset they will come out. I must go out. It is necessary that I go out (subj. pr.)

To go or come out, *uscire;* to hear, *udire;* you must hear: it is necessary that you hear (subj. pr.); it is necessary, *bisogna;* the whole world, *il mondo intero;* bird, *uccello;* only, (not but,) *non — che;* night, *notte;* after sunset, *a sera.*

We do not succeed because we do not try. If they try they will succeed. He tries, but does not succeed. I do not think that he hears (subj. pr.) you. If he heard (subj. imp.) you he would answer. Let them answer if they hear (ind. pr.) Answer (thou) if thou hearest.

To succeed, *riuscire;* to try, *provare;* to think, *credere;* to hear, *udire;* to answer, *rispondere.*

Let them fulfil their duties. A ghost appears to me every night, which fills me with (of) terror. Come (thou), let us fly together. The Romans die and fly not. He who flies, conquers. Help (thou) me or I die. Save us or we die.

To fulfil, *adempire;* to fill, *empire;* to come, *venire;* to fly, *fuggire;* to die, *morire;* to conquer, *vincere;* to help, *soccorrere;* to save, *salvare;* duty, *dovere;* night, *notte;* terror, *terrore.*

They do not succeed now as they did (succeed) once. The way is open if thou darest. What way is closed for (to) a man who dares? How many die without hope. These poor girls fall into consumption. When he sees me he turns pale.

To succeed, *riuscire;* to dare, *ardire;* to close, *chiudere;* to fall into consumption, *intisichire;* to turn pale, *impallidire;* now, *ora;* once, *una volta;* way, *via;* how many, *quanti;* hope, *speranza;* girl, *ragazza;* poor, *povero.*

XXII.—DEFECTIVE VERBS.

1. *Angere,* to afflict.
Pr. Ind. *ange,* he afflicts. (No other tense or person.)
2. *Algere,* to freeze.
Pret. *alsi, algesti,* &c. (No other tense.)
3. *Arrogere,* to add. Ger. *arrogendo.* P. P. *arroso, or arroto.*
Pr. Ind. *arroge,* he adds. Pret. *arrose,* he added. (No other tense.)
4. *Calére,* to care (used impersonally with dative pronouns.)
   Ex. *Mi cale,* I care; *ti cale,* thou carest, &c.
Pr. Ind. *cale.* Imp. *caleva.* Pret. *calse.*
Subj. Pr. *caglia.* Imp. *calesse;* (in compound tenses conjugated with *essere,* as *mi è caluto,* I have cared.)
5. *Colere,* to worship, *or* revere.
Pr. Ind. *colo,* I revere; *cole,* he reveres. (No other person or tense.)
6. *Estollere,* to raise, *or* exalt.
Pr. Ind. *estolle,* he raises. (No other tense or person.)
7. *Fiedere,* to smite. Ger. *fiedendo.*
Pr. Ind. *fiedo, fiedi, fiede;* pl. *fiedono.* Imp. *fiedeva.*
Pret. *fiedei.*
Subj. Pr. *fieda,* &c. Imp. *fiedessi,* &c.
8. *Gire,* to go. P. P. *gito.*
Pr. Ind. *gite,* you go. Imp. *giva,* &c. Pret. *gii, gisti,* &c.

Fut. *girò*, &c. Cond. *girei*, &c.
Imper. *giamo*, let us go. Subj. Pr. *giamo*, we may go; *giate*, you may go.
Imperf. *gissi*, &c. (otherwise defective.)
9. *Ire*, to go. P. P. *ito*.
Pr. Ind. *ite*, you go. Imp. *iva, ivi, iva;* pl. *ivano*.
Fut. *iremo, irete, iranno*. Imper. *ite*, go ye.
10. *Licere*, or *lecere*, to be lawful.
Pr. Ind. *lice*, or *lece*, it is lawful. (No other tense or person.)
11. *Molcere*, to soothe. Ger. *molcendo*.
Pr. Ind. *molci*, thou soothest; *molce*, he soothes.
Imp. *molceva*, &c.
Subj. Im. *molcessi*, &c. (Otherwise defective.)
12. *Olire*, to be fragrant.
Imp. Ind. *oliva*, &c.; plur. *olivano*. (No other tense.)
13. *Solére*, to be wont. (See Irregular Verbs, second conjugation.)
14. *Riedere*, to return.
Pr. Ind. *riedi*, thou returnest; *riede*, he returns; *riedono*, they return.
Subj. Pr. *rieda*, 3 pers.; plu. *riedano*. (Otherwise defective.)
15. *Tangere*, to touch.
Pr. Ind. *tange*, he touches. (No other tense or person.)
16. *Urgere*, to urge. Ger. *urgendo*.
Pr. Ind. *urge*, he presses. Imp. *urgeva*; plur. *urgevano*.
Subj. Im. *urgesse*, *urgessero*.

Exercise.

I usually go to bed at twelve. They usually dine at six. I used to ride morning and afternoon. I do not care for him. I have your happiness at heart. Take to heart the welfare of your children. I did not think you cared (subj. imp.) so much for it.

Usually to do a thing, *solere fare una cosa;* to go to bed, *andare a letto;* to dine, *pranzare;* to use, *solere;* to ride, *cavalcare;* to care for, *calere di;* to have, or take to heart, *calere*; to care for, *calere di*. Ex. I care for you, *mi cale di voi*; you care for me, *vi cale di me*; morning, *mattina*; afternoon, *dopo pranzo*; happiness, *felicità*; well being, *bene*; child, *figlio*; so much, *tanto*. How every flower sweetly smelt. Your misery does not concern me. I never cared for thy love. Do not think that I care for it. Who assuages, oh! poor prisoner, thy gloomy cares? Thus does he raise his great forehead and his great horns. Men are wont sooner to forget favours than injuries.

To smell, *olire*; to concern, *tangere*; to care, *calere*; to think, *credere*; to assuage, *molcere*; to raise, *estollere*; to be wont, *solere*; to forget, *dimenticare*; how, *come*; flower, *fiore*; sweetly, *soavemente*; misery, *miseria*; love, *amore*; never, *non — mai*; poor, *misero*; prisoner, *prigione*; gloomy, *tetro*; care, *cura*; thus, *cosi*; his great forehead, *la gran fronte*; his great horns, *le gran corna*; favour, *beneficio*; injury, *ingiuria*.

XXIII.—PREPOSITIONS.

1. The Prepositions have many idiomatic peculiarities, only to be learned by practice and example.

Di,—of.

Examples.

la casa di mio padre,	my father's house.
la corona di ferro,	the iron crown.
è ora di pranzo,	it is dinner time.
non mi fido di lui,	I do not trust him.
domandano di voi,	they ask *for* you.
partii di Parigi,	I set out *from* Paris.
vengo di casa,	I come *from* home.
di giorno in giorno,	*from* day *to* day.

L

punito di *morte,*	punished *with* death.
accusato di *furto,*	charged *with* theft.
provveduto di *denari,*	supplied *with* money.
ferito di *spada,*	wounded *with a* sword.
mi fece d' *occhio,*	he winked *at* me.
gli feci di *cappello,*	I took off my hat *to* him.
levatevelo di *dosso,*	take it off *from* you.
toglietevelo di *testa,*	get it *out of* your head.
più bella di *voi,*	handsomer *than* you.
godo di *vedervi,*	I rejoice *to* see you.
avviene di *rado,*	it seldom happens.
parlò di *forza,*	he spoke forcibly.

2. *A,* or *ad,*—to, *or* at.

andiamo a *Roma,*	we go *to* Rome.
date a *Cesare,*	give *to* Cæsar.
venne a *trovarmi,*	he came *to* see me.
l' ho mandato a *cercare,*	I have sent to look *for* him.
avvicinati a *me,*	come near me.
si appoggia al *muro,*	he leans *against the* wall.
dirimpetto all' *ospedale,*	opposite *to* the hospital.
pon mente a *ciò ch' io dico,*	mind what I say.
furon tagliati a *pezzi,*	they were cut to pieces.
vanno a *due* a *due,*	they go two *by* two.
l' ho imparato a *mente,*	I have learned it *by* heart.
muoiono a *migliaia,*	they die *by* thousands.
state all' *erta,*	be *on the* watch.
camminano al *buio,*	they walk *in the* dark.
non opro a *caso,*	I do not act *by* chance.
stette a *bocca aperta,*	he stood *with* open mouth.
cammina a *capo chino,*	he walks *with* downcast head.
l' ho letto alla *sfuggita,*	I have run over it.
lo fece all' *impensata,*	he did it thoughtlessly.
va tutto alla *peggio,*	all goes for the worst.
una scala a *chiocciola,*	a winding staircase.
è fatto a *vite,*	it is made screw-wise.
vestita alla *Francese,*	dressed *in the* French fashion.

PREPOSITIONS.

dipinto a maraviglia,	painted wonderfully well.
lo fece a mia richiesta,	he did it *by* my request.
se lo ebbe a male,	he took it ill.

3. *Da*,—from, *or* by.

partii da Parigi,	I set out *from* Paris.
vengo da casa,	I come *from* home.
lontano dalla patria,	far *from* one's country.
lodato da tutti,	praised *by* every one.
discordo da voi,	I differ *with* you.
dipende dal marito,	she depends *on* her husband.
guardatevi da lui,	beware *of* him.
venite da me.	come *to* me (to my house).
passate da casa mia,	pass *by* (or come *to*) my house.
da noi non si fa,	this is not done *amongst* us.
l' ho fatto da me,	I have done it *by* myself.
vi parlo da amico,	I speak to you *as a* friend.
un cappello da signore,	a hat *fit for a* gentleman.
una giovane da marito,	a girl *in* a marriageable age.
datemi da pranzo,	give me something *for* dinner.
avete niente da mangiare?	have you anything *to* eat?
non ho da servirvi,	{ I have not *the means to* serve you.
egli non è da temere,	he is not *to* be feared.
che c' è da ridere?	what is there *to* laugh at?
è fuggito da quella parte,	he ran that way.
diteglielo da parte mia,	tell it him *in* my name.
avete carta da scrivere?	have you writing paper?
è tutta roba da vendere,	all this is *to* be sold.
è una scena da commedia,	it is a scene *for* a comedy.
l' errare è da uomo,	to err is human.
non son cose da pari vostro,	{ these are not things *for* one like you.
vi sarebbe che dire da ambe le parti,	there is something to say *on* both sides.

4. *Per*,—for, *or* by.

l' ho fatto per voi,	{ I have done it *for* you (for your sake).

ho viaggiato per *Francia*,	I have travelled *about* in France.
l' ho detto per *ischerzo*,	I have said it *as* a jest.
ciò che per *lui si è fatto*,	what has been done *by* him.
diteglielo per *parte mia*,	tell it him *in* my name.
fu lasciato per *morto*,	he was left *as* dead.
passa per *onest' uomo*,	he is thought to be an honest man.
andate pei *fatti vostri*,	go *about* your business.
sto per *partire*,	I am *about to* set out.
non lo conto per *nulla*,	I reckon him *as* nothing.
per *me ve lo cedo*,	*as for* me I give it up to you.
piovve per *tre giorni*,	it rained *for* three days.
per quanto *vi affatichiate*,	*however* you may exert yourself.

5. *Con*,—with, *or* by.

ha fatto pace col *nemico*,	he has made peace *with* the enemy.
è uscita col *servo*,	she is gone out *with* her servant.
lo fo con *piacere*,	I do it *with* pleasure.
leggo cogli *occhiali*,	I read *with* spectacles.
si distingue coi *suoi talenti*,	he distinguishes himself *by* his talents.
l' ottiene colla *pazienza*,	he obtains it *by* his patience.
supplisce col *coraggio*,	he makes up *by* courage.

6. *In*,—in, into, *or* at.

dimora in *città*,	he lives *in* town.
avvenne in *Marzo*,	it happened *in* March.
è andato in *campagna*,	he is gone *into the* country.
il pranzo è in *tavola*,	dinner is *on the* table.
è caduto in *terra*,	he is fallen *to the* ground.
furon fatti in *pezzi*,	they were cut *to* pieces.
la flotta è in *mare*,	the fleet is *at* sea.
mettetevelo in *tasca*,	put it *in* your pocket.
ha il cappello in *testa*,	he has his hat *on*.
tutti gli occhi eran fissi in *lui*,	all eyes were fixed upon him.
morto in *età di venti anni*,	died *at* the age of twenty.

in *punta di piedi*,	*on* tiptoe.
non ho denari in *dosso*,	I have no money *upon* me.

7. *Tra*, or *fra*,—among, or between.

fra *due muri*,	*between* two walls.
tra *il quinto di e il sesto*,	*between* the fifth and sixth day.
tra *i fiori e l' erba*,	*amongst* the flowers and the grass.
fra *tre giorni*,	*within* three days.
dissi fra *me*,	I said *within* myself.
lo incontrò fra *via*,	she met him *on* the way.
tra *viva e morta*,	half-alive half-dead.
tra *l' una cosa e l' altra io non sapeva che fare*,	*what with* one thing and the other I did not know what to do.

8. *Su*, or *sopra*,—on, upon, above.

la città è posta sul *monte*,	the town is situate *on* the hill.
la stimo sovra *ogni altra cosa*,	I value her *above* all things.
andò su per *la montagna*,	he went *up* to the mountain.
vengono su per *le scale*,	they are coming *up the* staircase.
col peso in sulle *spalle*,	with the burden *on* his shoulders.
sul *far del giorno*,	*at* break of day.
in sull' *imbrunire*,	*at* dusk.
memorie sulla *Rivoluzione Francese*; or, *intorno alla Rivoluzione Francese*,	memoirs *on the* French Revolution.

9. Other prepositions.

senza *danaro*,	*without* money.
senza di *me*,	*without* me.
dopo *pranzo*,	*after* dinner.
dopo di *me*,	*after* me.
prima di *me*,	*before* me (in time).
avanti di *me*, innanzi a *me*,	*before* me (in my presence).

prima di *tutto*,	*before* all (in the first place).
prima di *credere*,	*before* believing.
prima dell' *alba*,	
avanti l' *alba*,	*before* dawn.
innanzi l' *alba*,	
incontro a *me*,	*against* me.
contro di *me*,	
contro il *nemico*,	*against the* enemy.
contro al *nemico*,	
dietro la *porta*,	*behind the* door.
dietro alla *porta*,	
entro le *mura*,	*within the* walls.
dentro alle *mura*,	
in mezzo alla *strada*,	*in the middle of the* street.
in mezzo della *strada*,	
accanto al *letto*,	*beside the* bed.
allato al *marito*,	*beside her* husband.
vicino a *casa*,	*near* home.
presso il *fuoco*,	
presso al *fuoco*,	*near the* fire.
presso del *fuoco*,	
verso me,	
verso a me,	*towards* me.
verso di me,	
di là dalle *Alpi*,	*beyond the* Alps.
di quà dal *Reno*,	*this side the* Rhine.
oltre a *ciò*,	*besides* this.
più della *metà*,	*more than* half.
vicino al *mare*,	
presso al *mare*,	*near the* sea, on the sea, &c.
in riva al *mare*,	
lungo il *fiume*,	*along the* river, &c. &c. &c.

Exercise.

We expect him from day to day. What am I charged with? I write with steel pens. Trust me. She had on her head a wreath of roses. Come to me at the midnight hour. He was wounded by a hundred thrusts. A friend of the house.

To expect, *aspettare;* day, *giorno;* to charge, *accusare;* to write, *scrivere;* pen, *penna;* steel, *acciaio;* to trust, *fidarsi;* wreath, *ghirlanda;* rose, *rosa;* to come, *venire;* midnight, *mezzanotte;* hour, *ora;* to wound, *ferire;* thrust, *punta;* friend, *amico;* house, *casa.*

Tell him to come at noon. Are we far from London? He was forsaken by all his friends. I have learned it by heart. He behaves as a gentleman. Give me some supper. I have some money to give you.

To tell, *dire;* to come, *venire;* noon, *mezzogiorno;* far, *lontano;* London, *Londra;* to forsake, *abbandonare;* to learn, *imparare;* heart, *mente;* to behave, *trattare;* supper, *cena;* money, *danaro;* gentleman, *galantuomo.*

Do not treat him in this manner. Treat him with kindness. You will know him by his deeds. He has succeeded by perseverance. House to let. Buy a saddle horse. He comes with his brother. All this is for sale. He died for his country.

To treat, *trattare;* manner, *modo;* kindness, *bontà;* to know, *conoscere;* to succeed, *riuscire;* perseverance, *perseveranza;* deed, *azione;* house, *casa;* to let, *affittare;* to buy, *comprare;* saddle, *sella;* horse, *cavallo;* to come, *venire;* brother, *fratello;* all this is, *è tutta roba;* to sell, *vendere;* to die, *morire;* one's country, *patria.*

He comes to town to-morrow. We go to the country in autumn. The English are strong by land and sea. Take this purse and put it in your pocket. All my friends are in town. Tell it him in my name. You cannot go by water.

Town, *città;* to-morrow, *domani;* country, *campagna;* autumn, *autunno;* English, *Inglese;* strong, *forte;* land, *terra;* sea, *mare;* purse, *borsa;* pocket, *tasca;* in my name (on my part); water, *acqua.*

He fell into the sea. Go about your business. All evil does not come to hurt. I have taken a house for a year. We were walking about the town. I have met him in the streets. They paid five crowns each. He earned two crowns a day.

To fall, *cadere;* business, *fatti* (to be used in plur.); evil, *male;* to hurt, *nuocere;* to take, *prendere;* to walk, *passeggiare;* town, *città;* street, *strada;* to meet, *incontrare;* to pay, *pagare;* crown, *scudo;* each, *uno,* or *ciascuno;* to earn, *guadagnare;* day, *giorno.*

How dare you look me in the face? Help me with your advice. Much did he achieve by his wisdom and by his valour. I read for my own amusement. What strange thoughts run through my mind! Do it for heaven's sake!

To dare, *osare;* to look, *guardare;* face, *faccia;* to help, *aiutare;* advice, *consiglio;* to achieve, *oprare;* wisdom, *senno;* valour, *mano;* to read, *leggere;* amusement, *divertimento;* strange, *strano;* thought, *pensiero;* to run, *correre;* mind, *mente;* sake, *amore.*

He is illustrious by birth. He is ennobled by his talents. He is famous for his high deeds. I come on your account. I cannot feign even in jest. Wait for me in the garden. He is known as a rogue.

Illustrious, *illustre;* birth, *nascita;* ennobled, *fatto illustre;* talent, *talento;* famous, *chiaro;* high, *grande;* deed, *azioni;* to come, *venire;* on your account (for your sake); sake, *amore;* to feign, *fingere;* jest, *gioco;* to wait for, *aspettare;* garden, *giardino;* rogue, *mariuolo.*

I have said it as a jest. You advise me as a true friend. I wish to speak to you *tête-à-tête.* He does not act as an honest man. You will learn the rest by practice. You will do it at your ease. The world goes always from bad to worse.

Jest, *scherzo;* to advise, *consigliare;* to wish, *bramare;* tête-à-tête, *da solo a solo;* to act, *agire;* honest man, *uomo dabbene;* to learn, *imparare;* rest, *resto;* practice, *pratica;* ease, *agio,* or *comodo;* world, *mondo;* always, *sempre;* bad, *male;* worse, *peggio.*

He will come within three days. Let this be said between us. Amongst friends one can speak freely. They come to us (at our house) every evening. Go to him. We dine at the Marchioness's this evening. He wavers between hope and fear. He will come without doubt. The body lay without feeling and life. I will do nothing without you. Far from the eyes, far from the heart.

To come, *venire;* day, *giorno;* to say, *dire;* can, *potere;* to speak, *parlare;* freely, *liberamente;* to us, (at our house,) (as in French, *chez nous,*) *chez da;* to dine, *pranzare;* marchioness, *marchesa;* this evening, *stasera;* to waver, *ondeggiare;* hope, *speranza;* fear, *timore;* without doubt, *senza dubbio,* or *senz' altro;* body, *corpo;* to lie, *giacere;* feeling, *senso;* life, *vita;* to do, *fare;* far, *lontano;* eye, *occhio;* heart, *cuore.*

XXIV.—ADVERBS.

1. Many adjectives become adverbs by adding *mente* to their termination in *a* or *e*.

Example.

lo vedo chiara-mente,   I see it *clearly.*
visse felice-mente,   he lived *happily.*
fu trattato crudel-mente,   he was treated *cruelly.*

2. Some adjectives may be used adverbially.

Example.

parlate chiaro,   speak *plainly.*
vivete felice,   live happily.

3. Some adjectives and nouns become adverbs by the addition of a preposition.

Example.

avviene di rado,	it happens *seldom.*
l' ho fatto in fretta,	I have done it *hurriedly.*
osservatelo pel minuto,	look at it *minutely.*

4. The following adverbs are in frequent use:—

non vi affaticate tanto,	do not exert yourself *so much.*
voi studiate troppo,	you study *too much.*
spende molto,	he spends *a great deal.*
guadagna poco,	he earns *little.*
mi preme assai,	I care *much* for it.
l' ho aspettato abbastanza,	{ I have waited for him *long enough.*
non ci penso più,	I think no *more* of it.
non potreste darmi meno,	you could not give me *less.*
non posso dirvi di più,	I cannot tell you *more.*
non posso far di meno,	I can do no *less.*
potrei parlar meglio?	could I speak *better?*
che può avvenirmi di peggio?	what can happen to me *worse?*
il malato va di bene in meglio,	the patient goes *better and better.*
va tutto per la peggio,	all turns out *for the worst.*
lo vedo sempre,	I *always* see him.
non lo vedo mai,	I *never* see him.
non gli perdonò giammai,	he *never* forgave him.
l' ho già veduto,	I have *already* seen him.
non credo già che venga,	{ I do not (*indeed*) think he will come, (expletive.)
non è già colpa vostra,	{ It is not (*indeed*) your own fault, (expletive.)
non lo sogna neppure,	he does *not even* dream of it.
avete forse *paura?*	are you *then* afraid? (expletive.)
verrà forse *domani,*	{ he will come *perhaps* to-morrow.
stette alquanto in forse,	he was *in doubt* some time.
venite quì,	come *hither.*
là era la fossa,	*there* was the grave.

ADVERBS.

ivi *giacciono le reliquie,*	*there* lie the remnants.
correvano chi quà *chi* là.	they ran about, some *here,* some *there.*
mia moglie è di là,	my wife is *there* (in *the next room*).
vi *sono bricconi anche* qui,	*here* also *there* are rogues.
vi *è gente* dappertutto,	*there* are people *everywhere.*
donde *venite ?*	*where* do you come *from ?*
dove *andate ?*	*whither* are you going ?
l' ho messo non so dove,	I have put it I know not *where.*
ci *vado quando posso,*	I go *(there)* when I can.
non ci *vengo se non m' invitate,*	I do not come *(here)* unless you invite me.
piuttosto oggi *che* domani,	rather *to-day* than *to-morrow.*
l' aspettiamo dall' oggi al domani,	we expect him *from* day *today, (daily.)*
non l' ho veduto nè prima *nè* dopo,	I have seen him neither *before* nor *afterwards.*
lo vedo spesso,	I see him *often.*
riesce rare volte, *or* di rado,	he *seldom* succeeds.
tali cose avvengono talvolta, *or* talora,	such things happen *sometimes.*
avviene di quando in quando,	it happens *from time to time.*
l' inverno passa presto,	winter is *soon* over.
verrò quanto prima,	I will come *as soon as I can.*
venite qui subito,	come here *directly.*
ci *arrivò* di subito,	he came upon us *suddenly.*
arrivò tardi,	he arrived *late.*
parlate adagio,	speak *slowly.*
fa fatto in fretta,	it was done *in a hurry.*
mi parlò a lungo,	he spoke to me *a long time.*
alla lunga *non regge,*	it does not hold *in the long run.*
lo supera di gran lunga,	he beat him by *a long distance.*
l' affare va per le lunghe,	the affair drags to *a great length.*
la lite durò un pezzo,	the law suit lasted *a long while.*

se ne andò per tempo,	he went away *early* or *betimes*.
non parlo a caso,	I do not speak *at random*.
fate da vero *o* da burla?	are you *in earnest* or *jesting*?
è difficile il far presto e bene,	it is difficult to do *quick* and *well*.
fate male *a non parlargliene*,	you do *wrong* in not speaking to him.
ha messo sossopra *la casa*,	he has put the house *topsyturvy*.
ho quasi *finito*,	I have *almost* done.
giuoca invece *di studiare*,	he plays *instead* of studying.
appena *vi arriva*,	he *scarcely* reaches it.
lo vidi appena *arrivato*,	I saw him *as soon as* he arrived.
voi lo pregate invano, *or* indarno,	you beg him *in vain*.
lo fanno volontieri,	they do it *willingly*.
ci vengono a malincuore,	they come here *unwillingly*.
vanno e vengono a vicenda,	they go and come *by turns*.
lo invitano a gara,	they invite him *by competition*, (they *strive with each other* in inviting him.) (French, *à l'envi*.)
si tien sempre in disparte,	he always keeps *aloof*, or *aside*.
per lo più *dormo bene*,	I *generally* sleep well.
gli uomini per lo più *sono egoisti*,	men are *for the most part* selfish.
non ci penso affatto,	I do not think of it *at all*.
non me ne curo punto,	I do not care for it *in the least*.
verrà senza dubbio, *or* senza fallo, *or* senz' altro,	he will come *without doubt*.
giacevano alla rinfusa,	they were lying *pêle-mêle*.
è alquanto *più attempata*,	he is *somewhat* more aged.

Exercise.

He walks slowly. Do not look at me so fiercely. He has served me faithfully. He advanced boldly. Can I speak more plainly? I love my children tenderly. I will give him my daughter most assuredly.

To walk, *camminare;* to look at, *guardare;* to serve, *servire;* to advance, *farsi innanzi;* to speak, *parlare;* to love, *amare;* to give, *dare;* can, *potere;* slow, *lento;* fierce, *fiero;* faithful, *fedele;* bold, *ardito;* plain, *chiaro;* tender, *tenero;* assured, *sicuro;* child, *figliuolo;* daughter, *figlia;* so, *si.*

How sweetly she speaks and smiles. I will tell you the thing minutely. When do they come? Where are they coming from? How many are there? (of them?) Where are they going? We expect them to-morrow. To-day is the last day.

To speak, *parlare;* to smile, *ridere;* to tell, *dire;* to come, *venire;* to be, *essere;* to go, *andare;* to expect, *attendere;* sweet, *dolce;* minute, *minuto;* of them, *ne;* last, *ultimo;* day, *giorno.*

Here lies a cardinal who did evil and good; but the good he did it ill, and the evil he did it well. I have looked for you everywhere. I can never find you. He is always angry. Perhaps he has very good reasons to be so (it).

To lie, *giacere;* to do, *fare;* to look for, *cercare;* to find, *trovare;* to be angry, *essere in collera;* cardinal, *cardinale;* evil, *male;* good, *bene;* reason, *ragione;* good, *buono;* but, *ma.*

I have scarcely a minute to lose. It is almost too late already. Are you then in a hurry? You ought not indeed to be so impatient. You speak much and think little. I wish you would speak less and think more.

To lose, *perdere;* you ought, *dovere* (condit.); to be in a hurry, *aver fretta;* to think, *pensare;* I wish, *volere* (condit.); you would speak, *parlare* (subj. imp.)

I can hardly believe it. They are rogues for the most part. They praise each other *by competition,* (outdoing one another.) They flatter each other by turns. So you have (are) come at last. The whole city was topsyturvy. A great storm suddenly arose.

To believe, *credere;* to praise, *lodare;* they praise or

flatter each other (they praise or flatter themselves); to arise, *levarsi*; to flatter, *adulare*; rogue, *briccone*; city, *città*; storm, *temporale*; so, *e cosi*.

He was buried as soon as he was dead. He is scarcely twenty. She is almost too young to (for) be her mother. She is old enough to be her grandmother.

To bury, *seppellire*; to die, *morire*; to be twenty (to have twenty years); as-soon-as-he-was (one adverb); to be her mother (to be mother to her); old, *vecchio*; year, *anno*; young, *giovine*; grandmother, *nonna*.

XXV.—CONJUNCTIONS.

in *città* ed in *campagna*,	in town *and* country.
e *per me* e *per gli amici*,	*both* for me *and* my friends.
o *vincere* o *morire*,	*either* to conquer *or* to die.
nè *per amore* nè *per forza*,	*neither* by love *nor* by force.
non so se vada o se resti,	I do not know *whether* I should go *or* stay.
lo credo se lo dite voi,	I believe it *if* you say it.
lo dice ma *non lo crede*,	he says it *but* does not believe it.
perchè *non mangiate?*	*why* do you not eat?
perchè *non ho fame*,	*because* I am not hungry.
ve lo do perchè *lo mangiate*,	I give it you *that* you may eat it.
non lasciavam l'andar perch' *ei dicesse*,	we did not cease from going on *although* he spoke.
bella ancora, benchè *vecchia*,	still handsome, *though* old.
sebbene *mi lodasse*,	*although* he praised me.
quantunque *egli si lusinghi*,	*however* he may flatter himself.
per quanto *ella mi biasimi*,	*however* much she may blame me.

CONJUNCTIONS.

pure *non mi lascio muovere*,	{ *yet* I do not allow myself to be moved.
non cedo però,	I do not yield *though*.
non ritratto la mia parola, anzi *la ripeto*,	I do not withdraw my word, *rather* I repeat it.
è pazza, anzi *pazzissima*,	she is mad—*nay*, stark-mad.
io non so biasimarvi, anzi *vi lodo*,	I cannot blame you, *on the contrary* I praise you.
l' ho veduto, anzi *mi ha detto*,	I have seen him, *and even* he told me.
parlate pure *ch' io vi ascolto*,	{ you may (*well*) speak *for* I hear you, (expletive.)
dite pure *quel che volete*,	{ you may (*well*) say what you like, (expletive.)
non mi ha pur *guardato*,	{ she has not *even* looked at me, (adverb.)
tremo pure *al pensarlo*,	{ I tremble *only* to think of it, (adverb.)
eppure *si muove*,	it moves *though*.
non gli credetti, ma pure *mi commosse*,	I did not believe him, *yet* he moved me.
tu pure, *Bruto, figlio mio!*	thou, *too*, Brutus, my son!
mentre *egli parlava tutti lo guardavano*,	*whilst* he spoke all looked at him.
non l' avrà mentr' *io vivo*,	{ he shall not have him *while* I live.
è egli che si lagna mentre son *io l' offeso*,	it is he that complains, *whilst* I am the offended person.
si lagna quasi *fosse egli l' offeso*,	he complains *as if* he were the offended person.
siccome *non mi ha scritto*, *non lo aspetto*,	*as* he has not written to me, I do not expect him.
siccome *non me lo diceste*, così *non posso saperlo*,	*as* you did not tell it me, *so* I cannot know it.
tu giungi opportuno come *la pioggia d' estate*,	you are *as* welcome *as* rain in summer.

come *crescono i giorni la primavera*, così *si accorciano l' autunno*,	*as* days lengthen in spring, *so* they draw in in autumn.
ve lo do affinchè *lo serbiate*,	I give it you *that* you may keep it.
mandatelo tosto ch' ei venga,	send him *as soon as* he comes.
difendilo sicchè *sia salvo*,	defend him *so that* he may be safe.
tutto è perduto fuorchè *l'onore*,	all is lost *but* honour.
tutti periorono tranne *il fanciullo*,	all perished *except* the child.
non v' è chi possa salvarci se non *l' amico nostro*,	there is no one that can save us, *unless* it be our friend.
egli può salvarci quando *vuole*,	he can save us *when* he wishes.
può salvarci quando lo voglia,	he can save us *whenever* he wishes.
noi non periremo quando *egli* nol *voglia*,	we shall not perish *unless* he wishes it.
quand' *è così è subito fatto*,	*if* it is so, it is done instantly.
non può nuocermi quand' anche *lo voglia*,	he can do me no harm *even if* he wishes it.
mi difenderò purchè *mi guardiate le spalle*,	I will defend myself, provided you back me.
giacchè *lo volete eccovi la mano!*	*since* you wish it, here is my hand!
lo credo poichè *lo dite*,	I believe it *since* you say it.
dacchè *son partito non trovo pace*,	*since* I have left, I find no peace.
poscia che *fu morto un fratello, l' altro regnò solo*,	*after* one brother was dead, the other reigned alone.
non può regnar il figlio finchè non *muore il padre*,	the son cannot reign *till* the father dies.
in caso che *morisse il padre, regnerebbe il figlio*,	*if* the father died, the son would reign.
non succede il fratello ma bensì *il figlio*,	it is not the brother that succeeds, *but* (*indeed*) the son.

CONJUNCTIONS.

gli succedette il figlio, cioè he was succeeded by his son,
il Principe di Galles, that is the Prince of Wales.
lo amava molto, tanto più ch' he loved him greatly, all the
era figlio unico, more as he was an only son.
non so più che rispondere, { I know not what more to answer, yet I am not persuaded.
però non son persuaso,
non posso crederlo, per altro I cannot believe it, yet every
tutti lo dicono, one says so.
era il più forte, non di meno he was the strongest, nevertheless he was conquered.
fu vinto,
non siete degno di lei, ciò non you are not worthy of her,
ostante *prendetela,* take her *nevertheless.*

Exercise.

I tell it you that you may know it. Scold him when he comes. Why does he come so late? He is very unhappy, although so rich. He has left his umbrella, though it poured. He will repent (of) it, however.

To tell, *dire;* to know, *sapere;* to scold, *sgridare;* to come, *venire;* to leave, *lasciare;* to pour, *diluviare;* to repent, *pentirsi,* unhappy, *misero;* rich, *ricco;* umbrella, *ombrello.*

If I go, who remains? If I stay, who goes? I do not know if it is right. Neither is mine (a) theft, nor am I (a) thief. I will take both the nag and the money. You shall have neither the money nor the nag. Either the one or the other, I will have.

To go, *andare;* to stay or remain, *restare;* to know, *sapere;* to be right, *andar bene;* to take, *prendere;* I must have, *turn* (I will have it); theft, *furto;* thief, *ladro.*

How dull I am since my friends have left. I shall not be gay till they come back. We shall be merry when you return. I do not care whether he goes or stays, so thou leavest me not. I grieved for (of) thy absence, all the more as thou didst not write.

Dull, *tristo;* gay, *lieto;* have left (are departed); to de-

M 3

part, *partire;* come back or return, *tornare;* to be merry, *far festa;* I do not care (it does not matter to me); to matter, *importare;* whether he goes or stays (that he may go or stay); so (provided) to grieve, *affliggersi.*

This is my best, nay, my only friend. I wish, on the contrary, that thou tell me what I am to do. Do not insist any longer, for I cannot grant what you ask. I would not grant it, even if I could. He knows I have no money, yet he always begs me to lend him some. He shall not get any from me, nevertheless.

To wish, *bramare;* I am to do (I have to do); to insist, *insistere;* to grant, *accordare;* to ask, *chiedere;* to beg, *pregare;* begs me to lend (begs me that I may lend); to get, *avere.*

You will not be forgiven unless you repent. As they have gone away without leave, they will be treated as deserters. Since you forgive him, give him your hand. There is nothing to praise about (in) her, except beauty. Repent, that Heaven may forgive thee.

You will not be forgiven (it will not be forgiven to you); to forgive, *perdonare;* to go away, *andarsene;* to treat, *trattare;* to repent, *pentirsi;* to praise, *lodare;* leave, *licenza;* deserter, *disertore.*

If I could laugh I would (indeed) laugh heartily. Go (then) since you are tired of us. He speaks as if he were the master.

Laugh, *ridere;* heartily, *di cuore;* tired, *stanco;* master, *padrone; indeed* and *then* to be rendered by an expletive conjunction.

XXVI.—INTERJECTIONS.

1. Some adjectives, and even a few nouns and verbs, may be used as interjections.

INTERJECTIONS.

beato *chi crede!*	*blessed is he* who believes!
beati *quelli che piangono,*	*blessed are* they who mourn.
felice *il padre di tal prole,*	{ *happy* the father of such a family!
me lassa! *tu non vorresti, o padre ch' io piangessi?*	*woe is me!* you would not have me weep, father?
i figli tuoi? no non fuggiro, ahi miseri!	thy sons? no they did not fly, *alas! the unhappy ones!*
pietà, *Signore!*	*have mercy,* Lord!
animo! *datevi a conoscere per lo sposo,*	*courage!* give yourselves out as the bridegroom.
basta! *non dico altro,*	*it is enough!* I say no more.
viva *l' allegria!*	*long live* joy!

2. The following interjections are frequently used:—

oh! *che mai dici?*	oh! what sayest thou?
ah! *il cuore me lo diceva,*	ah! my heart misgave me!
ahi! *crudo sconoscente Saul,*	oh! cruel, ungrateful soul!
ohimè! *i fratelli!*	alas! my brothers!
ehi! *chi é di là?*	{ eh! who is there? who is in waiting?
ehi! *quella giovine!*	I say, young woman!
via, *non lo sgridate!*	come, do not scold him.
via, via! *che importa?*	come, come, what matters it?
eh via, *sciocchezze!*	oh come! nonsense!
su, su, *fedeli miei,* su via, *prendete le fiamme e il ferro, ardete ed uccidete,*	up, up, my faithful ones, come! take fire and sword, burn and slay!
deh! *perdonategli,*	oh do! forgive him.
dì su! *che vuoi?*	{ speak out, say freely, what wouldst thou?
orsù! *parliam d' altro,*	{ now come, let us talk of something else.
e così! *come va la salute?*	well then! how is your health?
guai a voi, *anime prave!*	woe to you! ye depraved souls!
che peccato! *così giovane dover morire,*	what a pity! to have to die so young!

peccato *che non abbia danaro*,	pity he has no money!
ah, *ch' ei pur troppo, a ricovrar de' suoi nemici in seno ei mi sforzava!*	ah he, too truly! he himself forced me to seek shelter amongst his foes!
oh! questa è bella!	oh! *this is fine!*
oh! questa sì che è bella!	oh! *this is indeed fine.*
oh bella! *che ci ho da fare?*	very nice indeed! what have I to do with it?
oh curiosa! *che colpa ci ho io?*	how very odd! how am I to blame for it?
è curiosa! *non ci aveva pensato,*	it is odd! I had never thought about it.
se ci coglie stiam freschi!	if he catches us, *we are in a fine mess.*
sta fresco *anch' egli, poveretto,*	he also *is in a nice predicament,* poor fellow!
evviva! evviva!	hurrah! hurrah!
viva *l' Italia!*	God bless Italy!
evvivano *i galantuomini,*	long life to honest men. Success to honest men!
che seccatura!	*what a bore!*
bagatella!	*a trifle! a little trifle!*
eh giusto! per l' appunto!	*just so! exactly so!*
ma bravo! ma bene!	*bravo! well done!*
tutti gridavano dalli! dalli!	all cried out, *have at him! give it him!*
zitto, zitto, piano, piano!	hush! hush! gently! gently!
zitta, *ragazza mia!*	hush, my dear girl!
zitte, *ragazze mie!*	hush, my good girls!
ohibò! *che discorsi son questi,*	O fie! how you do talk!
vergogna! *m' avevate promesso di non farlo più,*	for shame! you had promised not to do that again.
non tradirmi per pietà!	do not betray me, *for pity's sake!*
fate piano, per carità!	go gently, *for charity's sake!*
aiutatelo, per amor di Dio!	help him, *for God's sake!*

INTERJECTIONS.

abbiam di che vivere, grazie a Dio! — we have wherewith to live, thank God!
grazie, *signore, non v' incommodate,* — thanks, sir, do not trouble yourself.
tante grazie *del buon consiglio,* — many thanks for your good advice.
mille grazie *della finezza,* — { a thousand thanks for your kindness.
che bella cosa *poter dire: comando io!* — what a nice thing to say: I am the master.
mala cosa *nascer povero!* — it is a bad job to be born poor!
largo! largo! *che passa il re,* — room! room! the king is passing!
misericordia! che spettacolo! — mercy! what a sight!

Exercise.

Oh, merciful (was) she who succoured me, and thou (wert) kind who obeyedst instantly! Blessed be the day, the month, and the year! Poor me! my husband has forsaken me! Poor me! my wife has deceived me!

Merciful, *pietoso;* to succour, *soccorrere;* kind, *cortese;* to obey, *ubbidire;* instantly, *tosto;* blessed, *benedetto;* poor, *povero;* to forsake, *abbandonare;* to deceive, *ingannare.*

Alas! ill-advised king! Now, come! let him be dragged to death! Oh, Heaven! what hast thou done? Oh! glorious days of victory! Oh! my past times! Oh! (that) I could to-day meet my death here from the enemy's sword.

Ill-advised, *sconsigliato;* to drag, *trarre;* past time, *tempo trascorso;* that I could meet my death, *turn* (could I have death); enemy's sword, *inimico brando.*

Miserable us! what are we if God forsakes us! Oh! would it were daylight! Night, come, quickly yield to the blessed sun. Shall I see her? Oh! happiness! Ah, woe is me! who live ever in incessant darkness.

Miserable, *misero;* to forsake, *lasciare;* (would it) were daylight (sub. imp.); to be light, *raggiornare;* night, *notte;* to yield, *cedere il campo;* blessed sun, *almo sole;* happiness, *gioia;* woe, *lasso;* incessant darkness, *tenebre incessanti;* ever, *pur sempre;* to live, *vivere.*

Come! you have too long abused my patience. Hush, my child! Hush, my children! do not wake your father. O fie, for shame! have you forgotten the advice I gave you? Thanks, sir, a thousand thanks!

Too long, *troppo;* to abuse, *abusare di;* patience, *sofferenza;* child, *fanciullo;* to wake, *svegliare;* forget, *dimenticare;* advice, *consiglio;* sir, *signore.*

Do not torment me, for pity's sake! Send him away, for Heaven's sake. He is gone away, thank God! What a pity we did not think of (to) it before. How nice it would be if we could do without him! Pity it is (subj. pr.) so late.

To torment, *tormentare;* send, *mandare;* how nice it would be (what a fine thing!) to think, *pensare.*

It is odd! you always repeat the same thing! We are in a nice predicament if we must never open (our) mouth.

To repeat, *ripetere;* to open, *aprire;* mouth, *bocca.*

XXVII.—CONSTRUCTION.

1. The Italian Language admits of great freedom of construction.

2. It is, however, amenable to general logical principles.

3. The following are among the most important inversions.

(*a*) The nominative, or subject, may and should be placed after the verb.

i.—For the sake of perspicuity, especially when the same subject governs two verbs, or is followed by a relative.

Example.

lo dice il maestro, *e sa quel che dice,* the teacher says it, and he knows what he says.

ha detto il padrone *che non vuole uscire,* master said he would not go out.

è giunto un messo che desidera — a messenger has arrived who wishes
parlarvi, — to speak to you.
morì il papa e gli successe suo — the pope died and his nephew suc-
nipote, — ceeded to him.

ii.—By way of emphasis or antithesis. The emphatic word generally opening or closing the sentence*.

Example.

in questa casa comando io, — I am the master in this house.
se non lo vendete voi, lo venderanno i vostri eredi, — if you do not sell it, your heirs will.
a quel caffè non vanno che militari, — none but military men go to that coffee-house.
il pellegrino l' avrà sognato Carlandrea, — as to the pilgrim, it must be Carlandrea, that has dreamt of him.

iii.—For the sake of euphony, which generally requires the longest
member of a sentence to come last.

Example.

giace l' alta Cartago, — lofty Carthage lies low.
muoiono le città, muoiono i regni, — cities, empires perish.
verrà il giorno della vendetta, — the day of retribution will come.

(b) All other inversions may be reduced to analogous principles.

Example.

a popol servo non mancan tiranni, — there is no lack of tyrants for a slavish people.
I peccati o in un mondo o nell' altro bisogna scontarli, — one must atone for sins, either in one world or another.
dolce in ogni tempo è il benefizio, — beneficence is sweet at all times.
più che il dolor potè il digiuno, — fasting had more power than grief.
uomo per virtù celebre e per delitti, — a man celebrated for his virtues and for his crimes.
assai mi avanza in coraggio, in virtude, in senno, in tutto—David. — David far surpasses me in courage, in virtue, in wisdom, in everything.

---

* The effect of emphasis in the construction of sentences will result from the following short and simple sentences:—

i.—vostra sorella arriva oggi: that is, arriva oggi e non domani,
i.—your sister comes to-day: viz. comes to-day, not to-morrow.

ii.—oggi arriva vostra sorella: that is, arriva vostra sorella ma non vostra madre,
ii.—to-day your sister comes: viz. your sister, not your mother.

iii.—oggi vostra sorella arriva: that is, arriva e vi trova partito,
iii.—to-day your sister comes: viz. she comes and finds you gone.

tanto più irreparabile *sarà la vostra rovina*,	your ruin will be *all the more irreparable*.
il rival *salvar* tu dei,	*thou oughtest to save* thy rival.
il solo amico ch' io *vantar* potessi,	the only friend that I *could* boast.
l' abisso in cui precipitato lo aveano i suoi vizi,	the abyss into which his vices *had* plunged him.

(c) The following inversions are of such frequent occurrence as to become almost natural to the language :—

mi duole il capo,	*my head* aches.
corre voce,	*a rumour* is abroad.
nasce il sole,	*the sun* rises.
cade il giorno,	*the day* sets.
ci pensa il padrone,	*the master* provides.
all' avvenire ci pensano gli astrologi,	it is for astrologers to think of the future.
lo voglia il cielo!	may *heaven* grant it!
mi resta speranza,	*hope* still remains to me.
ci vuol coraggio,	*courage* is required.
ci narrano le storie,	*histories* tell us.
chi troppo *vuole* niente ha,	{ he who covets *too much*, gets *nothing*.
chi troppo *abbraccia* nulla *stringe*,	{ he who undertakes *too much*, achieves *nothing*.
comanda *chi può*, ubbidisce *chi deve*,	he who has the power *rules*; he who is bound *obeys*.
a buono intanditor *poche parole*,	a word *to the wise*.
a tanto intercessor *nulla si neghi*,	{ let nothing be denied *to so great an intercessor*.
ai voli troppo alti e repentini *sogliono i precipizi esser vicini*,	great and sudden flights are usually attended by downfalls.

4. The Italian delights in ellipsis,—that is, omission of words easily implied by the context of the sentence. We have seen frequent examples in the articles and pronouns.

Example.

si vede che siete poeta,	one can see you are *a* poet.
la processione era giunta in piazza,	the procession had arrived in *the* square.
hanno perduto il padre,	they have lost *their* father.

5. In the same manner auxiliary verbs are frequently omitted.

vedutolo, lo chiamò,	having seen him, he called him.
chiamatolo e trattolo in disparte, gli parlò a lungo,	having called him, and *having* taken him aside, he spoke to him for a long time.
sospirai la mia perduta pace,	I sighed for the peace *which I had* lost.
è inutile ripetere le cose dette,	it is useless to repeat the things *that have been* said.
il consiglio datomi dal mio amico,	the counsel *which was* given me by my friend.

6. The Italian omits the repetition of a verb altogether, when the English expresses it by the word *do*.

Example.

le mogli amano i mariti più ch' essi le mogli,	wives love their husbands more than these *do* their wives.

7. The following are amongst the most remarkable cases of ellipsis:—

fu punito di morte: viz. *fu punito* della pena *di morte,*	he was punished with death.
era di Maggio;—era nel mese *di Maggio,*	it was in May.
morì nel 1821 ;—*morì nell'* anno 1821,	he died in 1821.
è andato a cercare del medico;—è andato a cercar l' assistenza *del medico,*	he is gone for the physician.
gli han dato dell' asino ;—gli han dato il nome *di asino,*	they have called him an ass.
domandan di me;—domandan nuove *di me,*	they inquire after me.
il tavernaro racconta allo Scricca d' una: viz. *racconta* la storia *d' una che il morto suo marito appicca,*	the host tells Scricca the story of one who hanged her dead husband.

partii di Parigi;—partii dalla città *di Parigi,*	I set out from Paris.
in quella giunse il padrone;—in quell' ora, or *in quella* congiuntura,	in that moment, or at that juncture, the master arrived.
credo non verrà;—credo che *non verrà,*	I think he will not come.
come rimarrà Attilio!—come rimarrà stupefatto,	how astonished Attilio will be!
il cavallo spaventato a tal vista;—essendo *spaventato,*	the horse being frightened by the sight.
messomi in viaggio;—essendomi *messo in viaggio,*	having set out on the journey.
a lui tocca a comandare, a voi ubbidire;—a voi tocca,	it is his part to command, yours to obey.
è tanto avveduta quanto voi;—quanto siete *voi,*	she is as crafty as you *are*.
io posso aiutarlo meglio di voi,	I may help him better than you *could*.
voi gli parlereste più chiaro di me,	you *would* speak to him more plainly than I *could*.

8. The Italian has three modes of address :—The second person singular, *tu*, thou ; the second person plural, *voi*, you ; and the third person singular, *ella*, or *vostra signoria*, your lordship, your ladyship, &c.

9. The *tu*, thou, is used in cases of the greatest intimacy and connection, or else by way of anger and scorn. It is used, in all cases, in ancient, classical, or very elevated language.

Example.

a tua *madre non dir nulla d' una cosa simile,*	to *thy* mother *thou* sayest nothing about such a matter.
levamiti d' innanzi, poltrone incapucciato!	get out of my sight, *thou* cowled craven.
re, s' io ti *torno innanzi,*	king, if I come before *thy* presence.

signor, gran cose in picciol tempo hai fatte, { my lord, *thou hast* done great things in a short space of time.

10. The *voi*, you, (is used as applied to one person) in cases of incipient friendship, or towards servants and dependents. It is used in addressing kings, in a semi-lofty style, and in a tone of chivalrous courtesy.

con voi, *signore, si può parlare liberamente,* — with *you,* sir, one can speak freely.

vedete *se il pranzo è lesto,* — see if the dinner is ready.

i vostri *sudditi, o sire, hanno udita la* vostra *parola,* — your subjects, O sire, have heard your word.

damigella, sete *nostra,* { young lady, *you* are in our power.

11. The *ella,* or *lei,* is used towards persons placed above us in rank, age, or office, or generally towards strangers of gentlemanly station. It represents *vostra signoria,* or *la signoria vostra,* your lordship or ladyship; or else *vostra eccellenza,* your excellency; *vostra altezza,* your highness; *vostra maestà,* your majesty; *vostra santità,* your holiness, &c. The whole of the speech is supposed to be addressed to the *title, and not to the person;* and as the titles are all feminine, all pronouns *you* and *yours* are translated into Italian as if they were *it* and *its,* and are all feminine.

Example.

ella *mi* fa *un onore ch' io non merito,* { *you do* me an honour which I do not deserve,—viz. *it* (your lordship) *does* me.

io la *ringrazio infinitamente,* { I thank *you (it),*—(*viz.* your lordship or ladyship).

da lei *non mi aspetto che favori,* — I only expect favours from *you, (it,* &c.)

è questo il suo *libro?* { is this *your (its, your lordship's)* book?

come sta la sua *signora madre?*	how is *your* (*its, your lordship's,* or *your ladyship's*) mother?
l' ha veduta stamane?	have you (*has it, has your lordship*) seen her this morning?
quando spera *di vederla?*	when *do you hope* (*does it hope*) to see her?

12. The same form of address is also used in the plural, when *elleno* or *loro* represents *le signorie vostre*, your lordships or ladyships.

Example.

favoriscano d' accomodarsi,	be *so good* as to sit down,— viz. *let your lordships* or *ladyships be so good,* &c.
che dicono di questo tempo?	what *do you* (*they, your lordships,* &c.) say of this weather?
sono ai loro *comandi,*	I am at *your* (*their*) orders.

13. The following sentences will give further development to this peculiar mode of address:—

son venuto a trovare la signoria vostra, *perchè mi* ha *detto che* voleva *vendere i* suoi *cavalli, ed io volendone comprare, amo meglio venire a patti con* lei *che con altri,*	I have come to *you*, because *you told* me that *you wished* to sell *your* horses, and as I wish to buy some, I prefer to bargain with *you* rather than with any one else.
affidato alla gentilezza di vostra signoria, *vengo a pregarla di una grazia, la quale a dir vero non riguarda tanto me stesso quanto il fanciullo ch' ella* ha *commesso alle mie cure,*	relying on *your* kindness, I come to beg of *you* a favour, which truly does not concern myself so much as the boy whom *you* have trusted to my care.

CONSTRUCTION. 137

se continuano *il* loro *cammino,*
le signorie vostre *non*
possono *mancare di giungere prima di sera;*
or, more simply,
se continuano *il cammino, non possono mancare di giungere prima di sera,*

if *you* (plur.) continue *your* journey, *you* cannot fail to arrive before evening.

poiché ella *vuol rimettersene a me, io la servirò con piacere,*

since *you* wish to leave the matter to me, I will serve *you* gladly.

io mi rimetto a ciò che dice lei,

I will abide by what *you* say.

vedo bene che la *non mi crede,*

I see clearly that *you* do not believe me.

(*a*) *Lei* and *la* are pretty generally, though incorrectly, used in the nominative instead of *ella;* and *loro* instead of *elleno*.

ho veduta la sua signora madre.
Essa mi disse che verrebbe a trovarla in città, quando ella volesse promatterle di restituire ad essa la visita in campagna,
giungeranno domani le loro sorelle.
Esse le pregano per mezzo mio di far loro apparecchiare le loro stanze. Aggiungono però che esse non si tratterranno con loro che pochi giorni,

I have seen *your* mother. She told me she would come and see *you* in town, provided *you* would promise her to return the visit in the country.
to-morrow *your* sisters will come. They beg *you*, through me, to have their rooms ready for them. They add, however, that they will only stay with *you* a few days.

(*b*) In cases like these two last ones, great care must be taken to avoid ambiguity between the person addressed, and a third person referred to, especially if the latter be feminine. In the very last case, however, the Italian is clearer than the English; as in the latter it does not clearly result whether one or more persons be addressed.

LONDON:
PRINTED BY T. BRETTELL, RUPERT STREET, HAYMARKET.

BIBLIOBAZAAR

The essential book market!

Did you know that you can get any of our titles in our trademark **EasyRead**™ print format? **EasyRead**™ provides readers with a larger than average typeface, for a reading experience that's easier on the eyes.

Did you know that we have an ever-growing collection of books in many languages?

Order online:
www.bibliobazaar.com

Or to exclusively browse our **EasyRead**™ collection:
www.bibliogrande.com

At BiblioBazaar, we aim to make knowledge more accessible by making thousands of titles available to you – quickly and affordably.

Contact us:
BiblioBazaar
PO Box 21206
Charleston, SC 29413